DEFENCES AGAINST THE WITCHES' CRAFT

Defences Against the Witches' Craft

DEFENCES AGAINST THE
WITCHES' CRAFT

By John Canard
ENGLISH ROOT MAGICIAN

Published by Avalonia

BM Avalonia
London
WC1N 3XX
England, UK

www.avaloniabooks.co.uk

DEFENCES AGAINST THE WITCHES' CRAFT

ISBN (10) 1-905297-18-1
ISBN (13) 978-1-905297-18-4

First Edition, AUGUST 2008

Illustrations by John Canard
Design by Satori

Copyright © 2008 John Canard, Avalonia

All rights reserved. No part of this publication may be reproduced or utilized in any form or by any means, electronic or mechanical, including photocopying, microfilm, recording, or by any information storage and retrieval system, or used in another book, without written permission from the authors.

Defences Against the Witches' Craft

For Hilda,
Dame of the Wild Hedge

ABOUT THE AUTHOR: JOHN CANARD

Having misspent most of his youth in the Cambridgeshire fens, John met the woman of his dreams, who he still believes to be only part human and moved with her to Somerset (UK) to live the wild life. They live on a small farm where John spends his time tending a menagerie of animals and growing organic produce. He has always enjoyed writing, having previously contributed essays to HEKATE: Keys to the Crossroads (2006) and Horns of Power (2008). Defences of the Witches' Craft is his first book, he is also working on a number of other projects related to traditional magick, witchcraft and root cunning.

If you wish to contact John Canard, please write to:

John Canard
c/o BM Avalonia
London
WC1N 3XX
England, UK

Or email: jcherbalist@gmail.com

He is always willing to correspond with genuine students of the mysteries wishing to expand their knowledge of root magick.

Table of Contents

FOREWORD 9
WHEN DO YOU NEED DEFENCES? 13
ARE YOU CURSED? 23
PROTECTIVE CHARMS 34
HOME GROWN PROTECTION 47
PROTECTION OF THE HOME 55
ENLISTING THE DEAD 69
ASKING THE ANGELS 72
QUICK FIXES 75
DISCONNECTION 79
RETURN TO SENDER 82
POPPETS 89
CAUGHT IN THE ACT 94
CLEANSING & SETTING WARDS 97
HERBAL SPRINKLER; HOLY WATER 101
CURSE JUSTIFICATION 104
PASSIVE CURSES 107
CLOSING THOUGHTS 109
(I) PICKING HERBS PROPERLY 112
(II) EMPEDOCLES' ELEMENTS 116
FURTHER READING 118

Defences Against the Witches' Craft

Foreword

This book came about through my lifelong interest in the disappearing world of our parents and grandparents. As a child I was brought up in Cambridgeshire, in the fens, where the modern world has mercifully not fully eradicated all the old ways to replace them with meaningless and soulless technology, devoid of arcane symbolism or ancestral connection.

I always loved to hear the stories told by the old folk of a time when the myths and folklore still echoed around the trees and houses. Even the language was evocative. A man staggering home drunk from the pub was performing the witch's walk. If he had drunk too much he would have visited the witch's church (toilet) to urinate or throw up before leaving the pub. The frequency of the word witch in slang drew my interest. I still use some of the old words and phrases, liking to keep them alive, though now I am using them in Somerset, where I live with my beautiful wife.

You may wonder why I should have titled this book *Defences Against the Witches Craft*? Surely I am not suggesting that witches do bad things that need defending against? Aren't I a witch myself? Well no I am not really a witch.

I am an herbalist, and a magician, so if anything I guess I fit more into the role of the cunning man of old and my practices fall into the category of root magick as described by the ancient Greek philosopher Empedocles, who created the system of the four elements, and was himself a root magician (*rhizotomoi*). And of course cunning men were often employed to fight the malefic magick of witches, so this book could be seen as a modern example of this conflict. From that perspective, there is a whole range of techniques in this book, some of which are not gentle or nice, but which ones you use, should you need to, is a matter of personal choice.

Today if you mention the word curse, people will probably assume you mean swearing, or perhaps some historical example such as the famous *"curse of Tutankhamen"* or urban myths about sports teams being cursed. Although swearing is a form of cursing, as you are directing negative energy at a person when you swear at them, this book is concerned with the type of curses directed with malicious intent which are aimed at causing negative effects on the recipient's life. We are dealing with ways to neutralize or reflect the type of curse which would have been called *'malefices'*, or evil magick, in the past.

The truth is that throughout history witches are best known for performing curses and malefic magick. It is a simple fact that they have always done so, and there have always been ways to combat them, and people who combat them as well. The modern pagans and wannabe witches are pale imitations of the witches from even one century ago, who usually know even less about crafting herbs, plants and roots than they do about magickal practice.

However this is not to say that people who label themselves as witches today are not dangerous. Indeed the old saying that a little knowledge is a dangerous thing was never truer than in the internet age. Now any person with a grudge or a jealous personality can simply go online to find ways to try and direct malefic intent at someone. Mostly this will be ineffectual, but sometimes the depth of negative feeling in such individuals may cause an effect. In such instances it is good to know how to deal with curses, because they usually come from those very people who pretend to be sweetness and light, and behind their dabbling they are secretly festering with envy and insecurity.

So with some encouragement I decided to put pen to paper, and transfer some of the knowledge I have in my head and old notebooks into this book. To preserve old techniques and charms for posterity, I have tried to be as inclusive as possible.

In some instances I have reproduced charms I have been shown with line drawings, as the owners of the charms were not willing to allow me to photograph them. This may have something to do with a feeling that the charm would be depowered by such an action. Although I have digressed in a couple of places to discuss foreign techniques, the material in this book is almost exclusively English. I have drawn parallels to magickal practices in other cultures, but my aim was to concentrate on material I myself have experienced firsthand, or discussed in a great deal of detail with people who have.

I hope that you enjoy this book, and that you never need to use the techniques I describe. But remember that protection never hurts, and the wider your spectrum of magickal knowledge, the further you can see.

John Canard,
July 2008

Defences Against the Witches' Craft

Chapter 1

When do you need defences?

"Truly the entrance of assurance into the mind of man is difficult and hindered by jealousy."[1]

It is often said, with the occasional patronising smile of indulgence, that behind the most civilised veneer lurks the soul of a primitive. Such superficial statements fill gaps in conversations, usually in an attempt to appear profound or knowing. And yet, as may often be the case, there is more truth in this declaration of professed kinship than the speaker usually intends.

Whether the metempsychosis of the soul is from Egypt to Cornwall, or from the Amazon rain forest to London, scratch at the surface of humanity and the thin top layer of *'civilization'* soon peels away. Stories told by grandparents or favourite aunts, urban legends from the playground and older local myths of shadowy creatures from the distant past, these were the canvas of childhood as society continued to move from soil to sand, hiding from nature to stare at screens and play with gadgets.

---

[1] On Purifications, Empedocles.

When we find ourselves away from our comfort zone, in unfamiliar surroundings, with unfamiliar noises and smells, the superstitions of a thousand childhoods flood back into our minds. When we are nervous and ill at ease we shift our perceptions and start looking at the minutiae that surrounds us. Doing this is actually a way of looking through a door into the invisible realms, though usually entirely unintentionally. The heightened awareness, increased suggestibility and sensitivity brought on by the unfamiliar, or more scarily by a moment of shifted perception where the familiar suddenly seems unfamiliar, can trigger all of our senses, including the hidden or psychic senses. Because we are not used to our senses being so productive, and do not normally deal with a barrage of subtle signals from the psychic faculties, this can lead to an even greater sense of disturbance or wrongness.

How do you deal with a situation where you are overloaded with more sensory information than you can cope with at one time? The usual answer is a trance state. The same is sometimes true of when your senses are clouded by alcohol or drugs. This can lead to a paranoid state if you are not used to the sudden inner silence. On occasions when I have been in London late at night it never ceases to amaze me how people allow themselves to become so vulnerable through overindulgence and then scurry like terrified rabbits through the tunnels of the underground, nervously looking over their shoulders and around them any time they cannot see any other humans in range, picking up mixed signals from what is essentially an unnatural environment.

Paranoia

So what relevance do childhood and situations that make you paranoid have on cursing? Well the fact is that paranoia is the root of many perceived curses. I say perceived because this book is not written to encourage paranoia or make you think you are a victim, and so I encourage you to read this section, and appreciate that it can be an easy trap to fall into.

When one little thing goes wrong you grumble and let it go. When the second thing goes wrong shortly afterwards you say you are having a bad day. But if a third and a fourth thing go wrong, you might start to attribute more sinister reasons to your catalogue of misfortune. This is particularly true if you start the day badly, through having slept badly or having experienced nightmares. Such a jarring start to the day always seems to leave the door open to the real or perceived peccadilloes of the invisible realms.

How you react to a string of bad events will immediately affect the outcome of that string. If you laugh it off and behave positively, you are short-circuiting any negative contribution you are unconsciously making to the events. If however you complain and blame the universe, or other people for all your woes, you are reinforcing the negativity and effectively inviting more into your life. It is a clear case of like attracts like.

Sometimes there are random strings of negative events, hence the old cliché of *"it never rains but it pours"*.

Once you allow yourself to become paranoid and feel that someone is out to get you, every little mishap will seem to be the result of the malefic curse, and this will just become a vicious circle you build around yourself. This is basically a process of self-disempowerment, where you disclaim personal responsibility and allow yourself to become a victim.

In such a circumstance, whether there is a curse or not, you should immediately perform a simple curse-breaking technique, even if it is no more than laughing at the notion that you thought you were cursed. You cannot allow your mind to either attract negativity, or in the case of someone actually cursing you, to do their work for them. By removing the distracting idea or mentally putting a barrier in place you are taking control of a situation and not letting go of your power, which is what you relinquish the moment you become paranoid.

Remember that accepted paranoia becomes belief, and like ingrained dirt is harder to shift. Do not allow yourself to accept your paranoia, and especially do not allow yourself to accept other people's paranoia. When people get into a group the level of common sense is not the sum total of the group, rather it is that of the group member with the lowest level of common sense. People whip themselves up into a frenzy and allow themselves to be manipulated extremely easily when it comes to belief or attitude. This can be seen in extreme levels in large groups from football matches to political rallies (remember Nuremberg).

A friend told me the story of a woman who was a priestess, and was convinced that she was being cursed. Every Sunday evening, she insisted, her nemesis would curse her using the voodoo techniques she had studied. Every Sunday evening she felt bad and this was why. As my friend pointed out, this priestess would drink heavily on Friday, Saturday and often Sunday too, so it was no wonder she felt bad by Sunday evening. The only spirits involved were the ones she was consuming, not ones that had been sent by her voodoo nemesis to get her! But this priestess could not be convinced that it was the result of anything but the cursing. She had reached a point where she was actually defining herself through this imagined rivalry, which obviously made her feel better about herself. After all she was obviously important enough to be the victim of such a sustained campaign of cursing, and this blocked out any thoughts that might arise through the haze of alcohol fumes that reminded her she was wasting her life.

A person who reaches this point has clearly made themselves a victim, and will interpret everything that goes wrong in their life as the result of negative influence. Conversely when things go right they are ignored and the pleasure of good events, which could help boost their mind body and spirit into a positive state, is wasted, because it would demand change. Such people can be very draining, as they may demand your unswerving loyalty (to ensure you are on *'their side'*) and will define their relationships in terms of this state. In such an instance you should consider whether the best policy is honesty, or distance. Both of these may destroy the friendship, but sometimes you have to put yourself first.

Depression can result in a worldview which automatically takes the most negative approach, so be aware that if a person has been through a difficult time, or is prone to depression, that they may be more susceptible to the idea of being cursed. Obviously you would not want to abandon someone who is going through difficulties, but ultimately you cannot help a person who is not willing to help themselves, they will become parasitic if they take no positive action and instead choose to perpetuate their negative condition.

Too Many Coincidences

So you have considered events and you know that you are not being paranoid, and there have just been too many coincidences and things going wrong. There comes a point when even a skeptic starts to get nervous and look over their shoulder! So what should you look for to ascertain whether you have been cursed? Beyond the obvious signs seen in horror movies but not usually in real life, of grisly animal parts left on your doorstep, the signs are likely to be a bit more subtle.

If you have been cursed or magickally attacked by someone who has not left a physical sign or told you that they have done so, you must consider the subtle signs. The following are possible indicators of this:

⊕ Nagging health issues – if you suddenly find yourself being constantly at low ebb, catching every cold and flu that goes around and being generally susceptible. This may also extend to other people living in the same space, and to any pets you may have.

⊕ Sleep problems – nightmares and/or insomnia may both be indicators, particularly if you always seem to wake up around 3am, the time when you are at your lowest ebb psychically, commonly called *"the hour of the wolf"* for this reason.

⊕ Bizarre pet behaviour – do not underestimate the ability of animals to pick up on subtle energies. If someone is cursing you, then your cat or dog is going to suddenly be very keen to spend more time outdoors, and may hiss or bark at times in what seems a completely random manner at things you can't see.

⊕ Mechanical breakdowns – the number of items breaking suddenly rises sharply. This might include car problems, household goods such as computers, washing machines, fridges or cookers, light bulbs, fuses, etc.

⊕ Communication problems – suddenly you miss important calls, the answer phone goes wrong, your mobile starts playing up or dies, your computer starts playing up or your emails start disappearing in cyberspace.

⊕ Missing items – money goes missing, or important documents you need such as passports, driving licenses, bills you need to pay, credit cards etc.

⊕ Spikiness – if someone is cursing you and it is having an effect, you may well notice a change in behaviour in your friends and colleagues. This will be because they unconsciously pick up that something is wrong but do not consciously register it. As a result they may well behave in a negative way towards you that results in impatience, lack of tolerance and general spikiness.

This may seem like a horrendous catalogue of events to experience, and indeed if everything on the list happened it would be rather grim. However this list is meant as a guideline to possible indicators, so it would be extremely unlikely that all the events described would happen at the same time. If they did it would be very likely that you were being cursed. However the number of these that apply can be taken as an indicator of likelihood – the more that apply, the greater the chance you have been cursed.

So you have read the signs and decided that you have been cursed. Now come the questions of who has cursed you, and why? Almost inevitably it will be a person (or rarely persons) you know. People curse for a reason, whether real or imagined, and this involves interaction with the person whose perceived or real behaviour has caused the person to feel they need to resort to cursing. You should also consider the possibility that it is not a conscious curse, but rather a general wave of negativity being projected from the unconscious of the person. Resentments that simmer under the surface for years, which may even have trivial roots, can build into a whole torrent of resentment, like a grain of sand becomes a pearl through being an irritant.

Curses can thus come from one of two sources – a conscious and deliberate attack or an unconscious attack. The former will either be a curse that the person tells you about as a specific act of malice, or a curse that they hint at or you have good grounds for believing they have performed. If a person has cursed you, to try and get a psychological advantage on you, they will probably only tell you about it when you are alone, as witnesses would be likely to support you and shift the balance of power, and also could verify your story. Of course in the case of a poison pen, i.e. someone who communicates with you by letter or email or some other medium and tells you they have cursed you but is too cowardly to admit their identity, it can be harder to work out who the culprit is, though you can resort to mundane methods and so this approach may be less likely as it leaves a traceable trail. Remember though it is almost always somebody you are in contact with, if only peripherally.

Effectively the process of dealing with a curse comprises three or four stages. These can be summed up as Detection, Protection, Disconnection and Reflection. These stages can be likened to the elements as described by Empedocles. Starting in the south with Air there is Detection, then in the west you have Water for Protection, in the north you have Earth for Disconnection (walking away), and in the east you have Fire for Reflection (light is attributed to Fire). These attributions may seem slightly unusual if you are used to modern magickal attributions. However until the nineteenth century the common elemental attributions were Fire in the east, Air in the south, Water in the west and Earth in the north. I have given a simple explanation of Empedocles' attributions and system in Appendix 2. Each of these four stages of a curse will be dealt with in the subsequent chapters, giving you all the tools you need to deal with negativity directed at you.

Chapter 2

Are you Cursed?

"Enmity is the first of the elements."[2]

Although there are exceptions to this principle, such as God starting history by cursing Adam & Eve and the serpent in Genesis, it is true to say that most curses are not announced, they are detected. We have already looked at the sort of signs and indicators that can help you to determine when negative energy is being directed into your life.

Next comes the most crucial stage of the process – detection. This comes in two stages. The first is detection of the culprit, and the second, which is not always relevant and depends on the form of curse used, is detection of the magickal link to you that they have planted somewhere in your locale.

---

[2] Hippocrates commenting on Empedocles.

Detecting the Curser

Detecting the culprit should be performed as systematically as possible. Remember it is almost certainly someone you have met, but also remember that it could be someone with a real or imagined grudge that goes back for years, which you could be completely unaware of. That is why you should use both mundane and magickal methods to help you narrow down the list of possible suspects.

Start with the mundane, making a list of all the people you know, and crossing off those you are absolutely sure have no malice towards you. Conversely highlight those you think might do, such as jilted ex-partners, or jealous work colleagues, etc. Between these you will also end up with a probably quite large group of people you don't think would cause you any problems, but can't be 100% certain about.

In fact this exercise can be quite disturbing as you may realise how few people you really know that much about, or indeed care to know that much about. This can also be a good object lesson in where the energy in your life goes, as you can quickly determine how much of that energy is wasted (i.e. not reciprocated), and is actually a parasitic relationship you might be better off without. An easy test would be something like, the last ten phone conversations we have had were all made by me, and person x wasn't really interested in my life, only what I could do for them. If this rings a bell, then dump person x! They may not be cursing you, but they are being a parasite! Of course there can be exceptions, such as if person x is seriously ill and cannot easily answer the phone, but obviously common sense should be applied at all times. Common sense is one of the greatest magickal talents we have, and it is disturbing how many people seem to either lack or neglect it.

So now you have a list of possible suspects. It may be larger than you are comfortable with, but there it is. At this point ask yourself, have I covered all the areas of my life – personal (emotional), work, and also uniquely in this day and age, online. If you are involved in online groups or forums, particularly if you have ever been involved in heated discussions or flame wars, you also need to consider the individuals involved, even if you only know them by an online name.

Now we move to the magickal method. I suggest one of two options here. If you are familiar with dowsing you can dowse all the names and see which come out as still suspect after they are all dowsed.

Dowsing for the name

Write each name on a piece of paper, and dowse each name in turn to see which one(s) give an affirmative answer to the question *"Is [name] cursing me?"* For this method, I would suggest dowsing the entire set of names, and then repeating the process twice, to ensure consistency in your results, as dowsing can be somewhat unreliable.

Dowsing is a very simple process, which relies on the psychic powers tapping the depths of the unconscious to direct the movement of the pendulum. People often use a quartz crystal on a piece of leather thong or cord. However personally I would suggest the old art of dactylomancy, i.e. use your wedding ring (if you have one, if not another ring without a crystal or gemstone in it) with one of your hairs to hang it from.

The most important thing to remember before dowsing if it is not a skill you have already developed is to ensure you know which directions represent yes and no, which is clockwise and which is anticlockwise. This can easily be done by asking a question like, are my eyes brown, or is my name Zog?

If your results seem plausible, i.e. it points to a likely candidate and not half the people you know, then your dowsing is likely to have been a success. Or, dowsing being something of a dying art, you can use the more convenient option, the Tarot.

The Tarot Divination

Take your Tarot deck (I am assuming if you are reading this book that you probably have one) and remove all the Trumps and put them to one side, leaving you with the fifty-six cards of the Minor Arcana. Now remove the Court cards and put them to another side. The first part of the detection begins here.

Take the pile of Court cards face down, and shuffle the cards, drawing out the one you feel most accurately corresponds to the person cursing you. Remember this is an instinctive process at this stage. This is why you should replace the card and repeat the process twice more and record your results. This is the real start of the detection process.

The following results are significant and can be used to help you narrow down likely candidates for malicious culprits:

If you drew the same card three times, that represents your culprit, and you will know whether the person is male or female, and what elemental group their zodiacal sign is probably in (i.e. an Air sign for Swords [Gemini / Libra / Aquarius], Fire sign for Wands [Aries / Leo / Sagittarius], Water sign for Cups [Cancer / Scorpio / Pisces] or Earth sign for Disks [Taurus / Virgo / Capricorn]). The chance of pulling the same card three times from a set of sixteen cards is 1:4096, so it is very unlikely to be a fluke.

If you drew the same type of card all three times, i.e. three Queens or three Kings, then this is a good indicator of the personal type. I.e. King or Queen is generally a person over 30 years old, Princess or Knight is generally a person under 30 years old. The chance of pulling the same type of card three times from a set of sixteen cards is 1:64.

If you drew the same element all three times, i.e. three Water cards or three Fire cards, etc, then this is a good indicator of personality type. I.e. the person will exhibit characteristics consistent with the element or their zodiacal sun sign will probably belong to that element. Again the chance of pulling the same element of card three times from a set of sixteen cards is 1:64.

If you drew the same gender all three times, i.e. three male or three female cards, then this is a reasonable indicator of gender. The chances of this are 1:8, so the odds are still in your favour.

If the cards are completely random and do not seem to have any pattern whatsoever, be it of gender, suit, type or specific card, then the results are inconclusive, and you can either meditate and repeat the exercise, or move on.

If any of the indicators from the Court cards applied, you should be able to reduce the size of your candidate list accordingly. Of course you might not know all your friends zodiacal signs, but their gender, rough age and personality types should all be fairly obvious! Write the list of potential culprits on a piece of paper with space next to them.

Now take the main pile of Minor Arcana cards, the forty cards from Ace to 10 in each of the four suits. Make sure they are well shuffled, and that you thought about the culprit when you shuffled. Look at the first name on the list and draw a card from your pile, noting the card next to the person's name. Replace the card in the pile and give it a quick reshuffle whilst thinking of the next person on the list. Repeat this process until you have worked down your entire list.

You now have a list of names with Tarot cards next to them. Discard all the names which have positive cards next to them.

The cards which count as positive and are thus discarded are as follows:

Card	Swords	Wands	Cups	Pentacles
Ace	Discard	Discard	Discard	Discard
2	Discard		Discard	Discard
3		Discard		Discard
4	Discard	Discard	Discard	Discard
5				
6	Discard	Discard	Discard	Discard
7		Discard		
8		Discard		Discard
9		Discard	Discard	Discard
10			Discard	Discard

You will notice that there are more cards to be discarded than to be kept. This is because there are more positive cards, and also hopefully your friends would not be prone to cursing you! Any names which have cards that are not discarded are your remaining culprit list. Now your original list should have been reduced substantially in size, it is up to you to decide which of the remaining people would be likely to take such negative measures against you. When you have a smaller list you are more likely to remember incidents which might have prompted such extreme measures by another person. I recommend repeating the process to reduce your list size further, and then hopefully the number of people remaining should be minimal. Now it is in your hands to decide which person you think is responsible.

Remember that unless a person has told you that they have cursed you, the chances are that you will not have any proof. This means that you should not alter the way you behave around your suspect(s) at this point. You will obviously be more alert around them, which may well reveal subtle cues which point out the guilty culprit like a neon sign above their head, but it may not. The identity of the person is useful if you are reasonably certain, but what is more relevant is stopping the negative influence being brought into your life. This brings us on to the second form of detection, magickal links.

If the person who you believe cursed you is someone well known to you, then the chances are that they will have had access to your home. A person who does not know you very well probably will not, but could still have accessed your garden if you have one.

The Footprint

In fact your garden can be your ally when you are trying to work out who could be cursing you. If you can somehow persuade the person or persons you suspect to go into your garden, try and contrive to get them to leave an imprint of their shoe in the ground. You can then use the old charm of hitting a nail into it. If the person is a witch or has cursed you, they will limp in that leg. You will soon find out if any of your suspects develop a limp, even if it seems unconnected, like through an apparently unrelated injury. This is one way to narrow down your list of suspects to find the culprit. As is often the case when dealing with cursers, it is preferable if the nail can be a coffin nail, taken from a graveyard. This was obviously a well known charm as it can be found in one of the Grimoires, the *Grimorium Verum*.

I will illustrate the importance of the magickal link with a true story. A friend of mine, a lovely girl we will call Emma, shared a house with her boyfriend and another woman, we shall call Joanne. Emma had a Siamese cat which was very affectionate to her and demanding of her time. Her cat started being ill, and its health consistently declined. Nothing the vet could do seemed to make any difference. On a hunch Joanne did a Tarot reading, which said that the boyfriend was jealous and had cursed the cat. Joanne told Emma, who refused to believe her, and an argument ensued which ended their friendship. The cat died, and a couple of months later I was helping Emma pack her stuff to move home. Feeling something unpleasant where the cat bed used to be, I rolled up the carpet and found an unpleasant charm, created to kill the cat, and written in her boyfriend's hand, incorporating some of the cat's fur. Not only had he killed the cat that he was jealous of, but he had also managed to destroy a good friendship as well.

The moral of this story, apart from being aware of people's jealousies, is that curses are much more effective if the culprit has a strong magickal link to use as a focus for their malice. Additionally if they can plant such a link in your space, it is always close to insidiously feed its poison into your life.

Detecting Magickal Links

So the first step in detecting a magickal link, if one exists, is to look at your list of possible culprits. Are any of them people who have had access to your home? If the answer is yes then you must be aware that they may have either stolen a small and portable possession of yours to use as a magickal link, or they may have taken hair or any other personal item they could get their hands on. As an aside, this is why you should not leave your hair brush or comb in the bathroom where anybody can get to it, and why you always dispose of nail clippings immediately. On a slightly less pleasant note, you should also not leave used items such as condoms or sanitary towels around, as they give access to your blood or semen, the strongest of all magickal links. So-called primitive tribes are well aware of the power of bodily emissions and dispose of them rigorously.

If a person has access to your home, not only can they take things, but as illustrated in my story above, they can also plant things there for maximum negative effect. Whilst this may seem very paranoid, if a person is hostile enough to curse you, then their behaviour is not exactly in the friendly rational category! If any potential culprits have had access to your home, make a list of any rooms they were in or could have had had access to, and do a quick search of likely spots for planting charms. Remember that when people make an item to use as the magickal link for a curse to plant, they are usually small for easy concealment. This means that as people often behave in similar ways, there are ways to search to see if something has been secreted in your space.

Put yourself into the mindset of the person who may have hidden something. Time is of the essence, but the item needs to be put somewhere easy to reach, as it would be awkward to explain why they were e.g. under your bed, but at the same time somewhere you do not look that often. The result is that people often opt for places like under carpets, or between drawers, or in the bottom of a wardrobe, or under a piece of furniture that does not get moved often.

If you do find a magickal link that a person has left in your home, you have irrefutable proof that someone has cursed you. Such items should be ritually destroyed, a process I will discuss in the final chapter. Of course if a person did steal an item to use for a magickal link, they may have kept it at their home or on them, so they can regularly use it to direct negative energy through it.

Chapter 3

Protective Charms

"Cures for evils, whatever there are."[3]

Curse protection is a bit like insurance, you hope you will never need it, but it is comforting to have it in place if things go wrong. To that end it does no harm to have protective charms in place in your home even if you do not believe you have been cursed, which is of course preferable. Bear in mind that charms for curse protection are usually also designed to keep out negative influences generally, so having them in place is no bad thing.

Abracadabra

One of the most popular and effective protective charms has become a part of popular culture, through its use by stage magicians. It is, of course, the word abracadabra. Some people might argue that this has devalued the word and made it useless, but I would argue

---

[3] Fragments I, Empedocles.

that in fact the complete opposite is true. Show me the person who does not know the word abracadabra and associate it with magick! The origins of the word abracadabra are in ancient Chaldea, as it is derived from the Chaldean phrase *abradake dabra*, which translates as *"to perish like the word"*. The word is usually written, and then repeated in a downward triangle losing a letter each time, until it is just an 'a', and then gone, literally the word has perished. This technique of reducing word triangles is one we will come back to, as it is commonly found in the *Greek Magical Papyri*, an excellent source of material for the enterprising magician or witch.

```
ABRACADABRA
 ABRACADABR
  ABRACADAB
   ABRACADA
    ABRACAD
     ABRACA
      ABRAC
       ABRA
        ABR
         AB
          A
```

The word abracadabra is sometimes described as a palindrome, but this is not true as it is not the same when written backwards. It was made famous in the Middle Ages through the Abraxas Stone charm. Abraxas Stones were used to drive away demons and devils, and protect the bearer from witches and the plague. They were generally disks made from a semi-precious stone, usually agate, carnelian, heliotrope, jasper or onyx. On

35

the front side was carved a figure of the Gnostic God Abraxas, and on the reverse was carved the Abracadabra triangle. Abraxas was a god of light, and if you add the numbers attributed to the letters of his name they sum to 365. Thus Abraxas was a light god who could shine on you and protect you for every day of the year.

As centuries passed, the uses of magickal charms often shifted to suit the social changes that occurred. They were either forgotten and consigned to the scrap heap of history, or they gained new uses or forms and continued to be used. The ultimate example of this magickal adaptation is probably the canonisation of old gods and their inclusion into Christianity. Many an old god (and goddess) found their way into the church and continued to be worshipped in a different manner to their earlier form. My favourite example of this is St Christopher, hugely popular as patron saint of travellers, whose protective charms are worn by millions. How many of those people know that he was originally St Christopher le Cynocephalus, or St Christopher the dog headed. He was in fact a survival of Anubis, the protective psychopomp god of ancient Egypt in a different form. When the animal head was no longer socially and culturally acceptable, he went into a full human form and continued his existence within the pantheon of the saints. Though I believe the Catholic church has now decanonised him for some reason.

But to return to the Abracadabra charm, Reginald Scot mentioned its use in his book *Discoverie of Witchcraft* in 1583 as a paper charm against ague (malaria), and it was being used as an anti-witchcraft charm by 1700 CE, as seen by the charm found in St Michael's church in Cascob, in the border county of Powys in Wales. There it is combined with a long Christian charm full of biblical references, as well as the astrological symbols of the Greater and Lesser Benefics (the Sun and Moon, and Jupiter and Venus respectively). The charm is now up on the wall in the church for all to see (except perhaps any witches it keeps away!).

By the nineteenth century instructions were being given that Abracadabra should be written on a square piece of white paper, folded to hide the words, and closed with a white thread tied into a cross, and then worn around the neck from a linen ribbon. The popularity of this charm saw such instructions reproduced in works like Smith's *Astrologer of the Nineteenth Century* and Raphael's *The Private Companion*.

Abraxas Charm

I have also seen an example of the Abracadabra used in a charm in more recent years. My cunning dame Hilda, showed it to me, and informed me that it was an heirloom from her grandmother-in-law. It was the same principle as the Abraxas Stone, but on a piece of vellum. On one side was the Abracadabra triangle, and on the other side was a stylised figure of Abraxas, with the unusual feature of a Sator square on his chest. The Sator square is another powerful charm, with a long history, and some inspired individual in the past obviously hit upon the notion of combining them to increase the efficacy of the charm.

Whilst it is unlikely that the author of the charm would have seen the *Greek Magical Papyri* (it was only published in 1992), it is worth noting that there are a number of depictions of human figures amongst the charms in this work whose limbs and bodies are made up of sequences of numbers or letters.

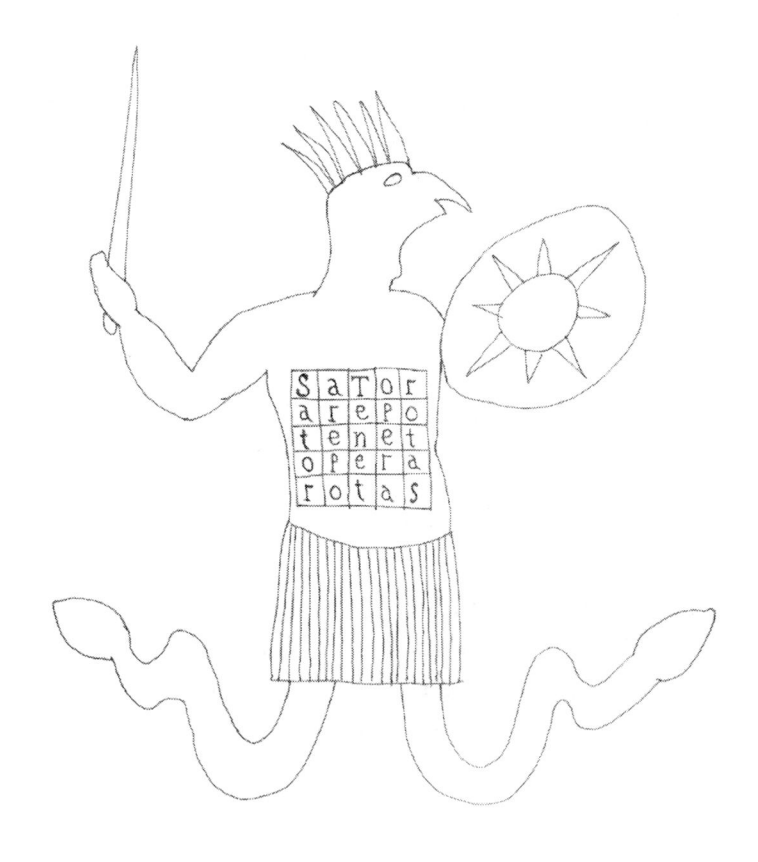

Thus the person had, whether knowingly or unknowingly, used an old technique which dates back thousands of years in protective charms. The Sator charm has been used a great deal for protection, and was considered particularly useful for protection from fairies. This is not to say it is not effective for protection generally, as it has a history of use dating back around two thousand years. As with the Abracadabra, the Sator charm has been widely used by people who did not know its origins or meaning, but who nevertheless believed in its effectiveness.

Adder Stone

Another old charm for protecting the house from curses and evil influences is adder or snake stone. It was said to be formed by the gathering of adders at midsummer, when they would writhe together in a ball and their combined saliva would solidify producing the stone. They were mentioned by Pliny, who called them by one of their other names, Druid Egg. In fact adder stone is ammonite, with a snake's head carved on the outer end for definition.

An alternative story is that the ammonites were in fact formed by the snakes which had rolled up into spirals and rolled over the cliffs at Whitby in Yorkshire, at the behest of the Abbess, St Hilda. As the snakes lay on the beach below their saliva caused them to solidify into stone. The ammonite has an ancient pedigree of use, being sacred to the Egyptian creator god Amun.

Its protective quality is clearly tied in with its spiral shape, and also perhaps the snake association. A spiral draws the energy into the centre and traps it, and it is an old belief that magickal energy (as well as ethereal creatures) travels best in straight lines. This is why labyrinths are used in some cultures as spirit traps, and spheres and eggs are often used as protective devices, as they contain no straight lines.

Charms for Luck & Protection

The aversion we have to bad luck and the chaos it implies in our lives is indicated by the popularity of good luck charms. These are one of the simplest forms of curse protection, from four-leafed clovers to charm bracelets, and have an empowering quality, as they help us feel in control of our lives again, bringing order back to banish the chaos. We use superstitions to avert bad luck, be it through casting salt over our shoulders, avoiding walking under ladders, or any one of a number of actions. Of course absence of good luck does not equal bad luck, and this does not automatically mean a curse is operating. If you have items that you believe produce good luck, then they may also be viewed as countering the negativity of curses. This can be seen in the past with lucky items being used to avert the *'Evil Eye'*.

The Evil Eye is a term often bandied around but what exactly does it mean? If you have ever been in a situation where a person gave somebody else such a malicious look that the hairs on the back of your neck rose, and somebody commented something like *"if looks could kill"* or *"they glared daggers"*, then you have seen the Evil Eye in action. It was originally applied to the conscious application of malice through directed intent by staring in a way that conveyed the malefic intent. This is why so many charms in the past had eyes in them, like the ancient Egyptian Eye of Horus, the Turkish Nazur Boncuk (*'Evil Eye Stone'*) and the Islamic Hand of Fatima with the eye in the centre. Now however it would be true to say that much of the malicious intent directed via the Evil Eye is probably not consciously directed as it might have been in the past. Rather it is often the consequence of emotional imbalance as a result of jealousy or anger or some other such state. What this brings to the fore is the state of modern society and the way people are often ruled by their unconscious drives.

Think of people as being like icebergs in the sea. They often believe that they only show what they think people want to see in their speech and actions. However people are aware of that submerged larger piece of the iceberg, which produces currents in its wake, these signs of its presence often being indicated by the body language and signals the unconscious gives out. Unless people have followed a path in life that involves self-discipline, which many have not, they will probably not even be aware of the negativity their unconscious can spew out like fumes from a broken exhaust pipe. Indeed they would probably be horrified if you even suggested that they were sending out large amounts of negativity, because they are completely unaware of what goes on beneath the surface in their unconscious minds.

Horseshoes

A good way to deal with such unintentionally negative people is to have something over your door. If a person has to pass under the item to enter your home, the message is being sent to their unconscious that they are entering into a protected area, and they are likely to behave in a much calmer way as their unconscious does not expend its energy in mischief. The obvious item to use here is the *'iron that moved'*, a horseshoe, which is imbued with the magick of the blacksmith, one of the great crafting and making traditions of our past, and definitely the most magickal. Horseshoes should always be hung horns up. The old explanation for this is so that the luck doesn't run out, and it looks like a lunar crescent. However when do you last remember seeing a lunar crescent that looked like that? No, in fact it resembles the horns of the bull, representing the power of the old horned gods of Britain, who were the hunters and tutelary guardians of particular areas of the country. The horseshoe taps into ancestral memory and has all the protective qualities that iron brings for dealing with malefic magick.

This connection to the horned god is hinted at in the old Cornish tale of St Dunstan and the Devil, which also explains why horseshoes are so protective. St Dunstan was a noted farrier, and one day the Devil approached him in disguise and asked him to shoe his *'single hoof'*. Recognising who his customer was, St Dunstan tied him to the wall and set about the shoeing, causing such pain that the Devil cried out for mercy. St Dunstan released the Devil, but only after extracting a promise from him that he would never again enter a dwelling displaying a horseshoe.

Horseshoes were also used inside the house as well as outside. An old aunt recounted the custom of *'hanging the red horseshoe'* to me a few years back. Wrap a horseshoe in red flannel, she declared, and hang it over the bed to protect the person using the bed from nightmares of any kind. She swore this practice was still going on in 1930s London, in the East End where she grew up. Today people are more likely to buy a dreamcatcher from a shop, but whilst I have no problem with this, essentially it is a native American version of a witch's cradle. As such I question the use of an item completely out of its cultural context when there is a perfectly good range of charms which have been used to good effect for centuries and are more connected to our psyches.

Nightmares can arise for a number of reasons, and it used to be believed that they were caused by witches riding on a person's stomach while they slept. Whilst this might not have been literally true, it does draw our attention to the fact that disturbed sleep, particularly over a period of a few days with nightmares, can be a sign of being cursed.

Of course it can also be a sign of excessive stress in your life, or unresolved emotional issues, so you do need to examine the likely causes before declaring yourself cursed due to lack of sleep. However to know what the likely signs are means you can also be realistic in reading events around yourself and not overreacting inappropriately.

Hagstones

The name hagstone for a holed stone is derived from its use to counter the aforementioned practice of witches with a penchant for nocturnal use of people's stomachs for chairs. In *Brand's Antiquities*, we find the following quote:

"A stone with a hole in it hung at the bed's head will prevent the nightmare. It is therefore called a Hag Stone

from that disorder which is occasioned by a Hag or Witch sitting on the stomach of the party afflicted."

Hagstones are specifically stones that have a natural hole running all the way through them, usually found in streams or rivers, and at the seashore, where running water has created the hole in the stone. They are also called Holy Stones, Holey Stones, Ephialtes Stones, Wish Stones, Nightmare Stones and Witch Riding Stones. They are believed to have the power of protecting people and animals from the powers of evil spirits and witches, and are often worn around the neck. In the past they were frequently hung on the key or door to the cattle stalls or stables.

If you are going to hang a hagstone in the house or wear one around your neck, a piece of red cord or thread is the preferred colour for its many magickal associations. Strings of hagstones can be hung by the door as an especially powerful protective charm. I have heard these called *'witches ladders'*, though that expression is one normally used for something completely different, being a device used by witches for causing negative magick. Hagstones are also thought to possess the ability to enable the bearer to see faeries, and be protected from their enchantments and glamours. Hagstones found at mounds or other such ancient sites are considered especially powerful. For a hagstone to keep its full power it should be found by the bearer or given in love.

Amber, which has become extremely popular in recent years in jewellery, was traditionally worn or carried for protection from malefic magick. This belief dates back thousands of years, with Pliny recording its use as an amulet to protect children from the evil eye. Considering the level of negativity in society today, it may be no coincidence that we have seen a massive upsurge of popularity in jewellery containing this beautiful fossilized resin.

Chapter 4

Home Grown Protection

"Earth causes its own substance to increase."[4]

A classic old Fens protection from malefic magick is to have yarrow (*Achillea millefolium*) around and under the door of your home. Yarrow plants growing near the door were thought to remove a witch's power if she entered the house, as was burying yarrow under the threshold. If by any chance she did make it into the house, the family would always have a cushion stuffed with yarrow handy to give to a witch, as if they sat against or on it, it rendered them helpless.

Indeed there is a whole range of plants thought to protect from negative magick and witches, as we shall now see. Several of the classic anti-witch herbs are mentioned in the old rhyme, which goes:

"Trefoil, vervain, John's wort, dill,
That hindereth witches of their will"

---

[4] Fragments I, Empedocles.

Dill (*Peucedanum graveolens*) was said to be a very powerful anti-witch herb, and this belief has even survived into modern times in the medium of television. Anyone who remembers the 1970s show *The Herbs*, may recall that when the herbs were bewitched by Belladonna the Witch, it was Dill the dog who resisted her spells and freed them from her influence. Nailing a sprig of dill to the door of a house was said to trap a witch inside if she was already in. This is worth remembering if you think a person you know has cursed you. Dill is also a useful herb for cooking and for cures such as dill water for gripe and hiccoughs.

Vervain (*Verbena officinalis*) [pictured above] has been considered a holy herb since ancient times, to the Persian Magi, the Romans and our own Druids. Its solar power was considered purifying, and it has been seen for thousands of years as a powerful protection from malefic magick, hence its name of Devil's Bane. An old protective charm using vervain is to tie a root you have gathered to a white ribbon and wear it around your neck. The root should be gathered with your hands and not using any iron tools, as you do not want to drain the energy of the herb when you gather it. Ideally a small offering should be made to the spirit of the plant when you harvest it as well.

Both vervain and dill were specifically mentioned as anti-witch herbs in the epic poem *Nymphidia* by Michael Drayton (1627), which may be the root of the old rhyme, or inspired by it:

*"Therewith her Vervain and her Dill,
That hindereth Witches of their Will."*

St John's Wort (*Hypericum perforatum*) [pictured above] is another powerful herb for using against malefic magick. Traditionally used in purification and exorcism, it has now become popular for a different sort of banishing, that of depressive states. So effective is St John's Wort thought to be that it has gained common names like *fuga daemonum* (*'scare devil'*) and *'Flight of the Devil'*. Another name for St John's Wort is *'rose of Sharon'*, and this name found in the Song of Solomon 2:1, may explain why the leaves were used as bookmarks in bibles in the past, a practice which presumably would be believed to further sanctify and empower them for use as a protection. Hanging St John's Wort around the house is believed to be a very effective protection from any negative magick or creatures.

Trefoil [pictured above] is simply another name for clover (*Trefolium pratense*). Clover is said to protect from witches and snakes, and of course the four-leafed clover is especially lucky and is said to possess the ability to enable the bearer to see fairies.

Lavender (*Lavendulae family*) is a useful anti-cursing herb. It was generally placed around the house, in sachets and pillows for the dual purpose of its lovely smell and also the now often forgotten protective qualities it imparts of deflecting the Evil Eye. This belief dates back to the ancient Tuscans, and may partially originate in the uplifting effect that the fragrance of lavender has on the person smelling it, but nevertheless it is a protective herb second to none. A lavender pillow or some under the pillow are good for banishing nightmares, and ensuring you are not susceptible to psychic attack in the early hours of the morning when your energies are at their lowest ebb. Of course lavender has a huge range of other benefits, such as being good for relieving headaches, easing insomnia, keeping clothes smelling fresh, etc.

The beautiful solar colour of the marigold (*Calendula officinalis*) flower averts the evil eye, and garlands of marigold may be hung around the door to keep curses and negative energies out of the house. Marigolds may also be carried and placed under the pillow for personal protection.

Hanging a bulb of garlic (*Allium sativum*) over the door is another traditional anti-witch charm to keep them from coming into your home. Forget the idea of vampires, garlic is used for protection from more down-to-earth malefic magick. An old charm recommends planting seven garlic bulbs around your home as a protection, and never again will you be bothered by the curses or spells of witches.

Gooseberry bristles (*Ribes grossularia*) were said to irritate witches, and have the benefit of producing fruits for you to eat. Rosemary (*Rosmarinus officinalis*), as well as being an aid to memory, was traditionally an anti-witch and theft herb, planted near the front door to keep such unwanted attention away from the home.

Of course the rowan (*Sorbus aucuparia*) is the anti-witch tree par excellence, and sticks of rowan gathered at midnight on Beltane Eve were considered an excellent protection from witches. Though of course as Beltane Eve is also known as *Hexennacht* or 'witches night', and is one of the two liminal times of the year when they are most likely to be out and about. A more useful home protection charm than the personal protection of carrying of rowan sticks on your person is the rowan and red thread charm, which we will discuss in the following section. Rowan berries, strung on a red thread and hung around the house or worn on the person are another anti-cursing charm. The tiny pentagram found in each berry provides a cumulative protection as you are then surrounded by pentagrams!

Ash (*Fraxinus excelsior*) also has a long history of power against witchcraft. In Somerset there is an old tradition of hanging an ash wreath from the nearest tree to the house as a protection from witchcraft, which by definition is clearly an anti-curse measure. The magick of the ash as the world tree can clearly be seen through its world-spanning nature. That the roots of the ash should reach deep into the underworld, place of malefic curses, is seen as a survival in folk beliefs across Britain.

Another protective tree is the bay (*Laurus nobilis*), also known as the laurel. Celebrated by the ancients as the tree of victory sacred to the Greek god Apollo, bay is also an anti-curse plant. Bay trees were planted by the front door in the Middle Ages to deflect both plague and the Evil Eye. This anti-curse property of the bay may still be seen in its positioning at the entrances to hotels and restaurants. From this perspective, planting a bay tree near your front door is a classic curse averter, as the old charm goes, *"Neither witch nor devil, thunder nor lightning will hurt a man in the place where a bay tree is."*

Perhaps the most versatile anti-curse tree is the Elder (*Sambucus nigra*). Elder berries gathered on St John's Eve (24th June) were carried for protection from curses. An old Welsh custom was to use an elder leaf as a stencil on the walls or floor of the kitchen, producing a protective pattern which averted the Evil Eye.

A dangerous herb with uses by and against witches is belladonna (*Atropa belladonna*). Whilst the berries have been used in flying ointments for their psychoactive ingredients, a wreath of belladonna worn by a person was thought to protect from curses. Obviously a belladonna collar should be worn over clothes, as you do not want the berries to be in contact with your skin where their poisonous and psychoactive qualities might be absorbed.

Rue (*Ruta graveolens*) is another herb found on both sides of the fence, as it were. Rue planted in the garden is said to avert the Evil Eye of witches. However throwing rue at a person and telling them they *"will rue the day"* is an old curse. The Herefordshire tale of the jilted sweetheart who threw rue at her former lover and his wife with the curse records that it was a very successful curse indeed!

One of my favourite flowers has a very powerful reputation as a curse-breaker, and that is the snapdragon (*Antirrhinum majus*). Wearing the flower in your buttonhole in the presence of the curser, or better still presenting it to the curser, will break their charm, and make them think twice about repeating their malice.

An interesting flower for protection is the speedwell (*Veronica chamaedrys*). Also known as *'angel's eyes'* and *'eye of Christ'*, the belief in this flower as a curse breaker is old and founded in its appearance.

To finish our garden we should consider the wonderful plant Hyssop (*hyssopus officinalis*). This herb has a long and unmatched pedigree as a purificatory herb, and as such is a very good one to have in your garden as its influence will spread to the surrounding area. It is found in grimoires like the *Key of Solomon*, where it was used for purification before ceremonies in ritual bathing, in association with the line from the Bible, in Psalm 51:7 where it says *"Purge me with hyssop, and I shall be clean; Wash me and I shall be whiter than snow."* This use of hyssop as a bathing herb, added to the bath, is an excellent way to keep your aura clean of any negative influences. Simply add some hyssop leaves to the bath, and as you bathe see your aura shining with a golden gleam, with no negativity attached to it at all.

Chapter 5

Protection of the Home

"Many are the evils that break in to blunt the edge of studious thought."[5]

A plant which should be grown around the door to avert the malefic magick of witches and others is honeysuckle (*Lonicera* family). Honeysuckle with its lovely fragrance is considered a lucky plant, suited to the attention of lovers, both to attract and also to protect. Juniper (*Juniperus communis*) is also a plant grown at the door, as it was believed a witch had to stop and count all the many leaves before entering. The smell was believed to keep away demons and negative energies, so it is a useful plant to have around!

A traditional charm which is said to stop a witch dead in her tracks is to hammer a coffin nail into the door frame. It is believed that they cannot pass by such a nail. The implication is that the combination of the iron with the blessing the coffin would have received during the burial ceremony would be sufficiently powerful

---

[5] Fragments I, Empedocles.

to counteract the magick of a witch. This use of iron is also seen in the hanging of the protective horseshoe over the door, as mentioned earlier and still seen surprisingly regularly. Other items to hang over the door include hagstones (also mentioned earlier) and the classic rowan and red thread charm, which may also be hung in a window.

Rowan and Red Thread charm

"Black-luggie, lammer bead,
Rowan-tree and red thread
Put the warlocks to their speed!"

I have seen this charm recorded on websites as *"Black luggie, hammer head, rowan tree and red thread, Put the witches to their speed."* However the *'hammer head'* is a bizarre inclusion and I think probably a typographic error by somebody who didn't know that lammer bead is a Scottish name for an amber bead (unless the idea is that it invokes the magickal power of the blacksmith, or worker of iron). This then clearly indicates the tying of a piece of amber onto the charm, which acts as a focus for positive energy, and makes sense with the protective attributions of amber being added to the charm.

There have been suggestions made about the mysterious term *'black-luggie'* being Jew's-Ear fungus or blackthorn, but I am not convinced. As I have discussed elsewhere, I believe this is actually the use of an old name for the Celtic god Lugh, who was also known colloquially as Luggie. This then indicates the sun (Lugh) in the earth, which also fits with the nature of amber as solidified pine resin, or literally sunshine give form![6]

People often make a rowan and red thread charm and then just forget about it. Do not fall into this trap! You should actually remake the charm every three months, burning the old twigs. At the same time you should also use fresh red thread and cleanse the amber. This can be done by burying it in the earth overnight (symbolically putting the sun in the earth, the black Luggie, as it were). Obviously when you pick the rowan is up to you, but I was taught that traditionally it is done on the quarter days of Candlemass (Imbolc), Roodmass (Beltane), Lammas and Samhain. This makes sense when you consider the nature of these days as liminal times when the hidden tides of the year turn and the subtle energies permeate nature more strongly, and hence more accessibly.

The cunning dame who taught me about herbs pointed out that the two most common times for picking protective herbs in the past were Roodmass Eve and St John's Day. St John's Day, or June 24th, was the old Midsummer's Eve before the calendars were changed. The quickening power rising in nature around Roodmass and the sun being at the height of its power at Midsummer show the outer manifestation of what is

---

[6] See Light in the Earth, in Horns of Power, d'Este (ed), 2008, Avalonia.

going on in the subtle realms. By picking your plants appropriately at the right times you bring some of the energy of the subtle realms into this realm, making the plant more effective as an apotropaic curse averter.

There is a variant of this charm mentioned by the witchcraft author Paul Huson used for luck with oak instead of rowan, with the charm hung by the door in the same manner as the rowan and red thread charm. Oak is of course the sacred tree of the druids, esteemed for its strength and seen as the king of the trees. The two twigs are bound with red thread in the same way, but the spoken charm is different, being:

"'Tis not oak which here I place
But good fortune – by its grace
May it never pass away
But ever in my dwelling stay!"

Ribbons are used in the old custom of dressing the birch tree nearest the door with red and white ribbons on Roodmass morning to avert the Evil Eye. The use of the red and white colours may be due to their alchemical symbolism. The leaves of an elder tree gathered on Roodmass Eve were also placed around the door or window as a protection from curses.

Hawthorn (*Crataegus monogyna*), the *'fairy tree'*, has a long association with witches, but was also used to avert their power. Pieces of hawthorn branch hung over windows are believed to keep witches and their powers out. However due to its fairy associations it is considered extremely unlucky to bring any pieces of hawthorn into the house. The white blossom of the hawthorn was thought to symbolize chastity, and also be a sign that Beltane was nigh. Combined with the thorns it makes for one of the most beautiful and yet prickly of trees, just like the fairies associated with it.

Flint Arrowheads

Flint arrowheads have been used in magick for a surprisingly long time. The Romans collected flint arrowheads and axeheads, known as *'thunderstones'*, and prized for their protective magickal qualities. Not only did they protect from malefic magick, but also from the spirits of the dead. Collections of such flint artifacts have been found in a number of Roman temples in Britain. This apotropaic tradition has survived in Italy, where children still sometimes wear flint arrowheads as pendants to avert the Evil Eye.

However, in Britain by the Middle Ages, flint arrowheads were being called *glossopetrae* and were thought to be the fossilized tongues of serpents. Flint arrowheads were sometimes buried under the threshold or walls of a house to serve as a protection in the same manner as a witch bottle. They were also thought to protect the building from fire and lightning, and this belief was found on the Continent, with flint arrowheads even being buried under churches sometimes.

Witch Balls

Another anti-curse device for deflecting the Evil Eye of witches is the witch ball. First recorded in 1690 though they may possibly be earlier, the witch ball, or wish ball or watch ball, was a large heavy glass ball, either brightly painted or with a golden or silver gloss. By the eighteenth century witch balls had become smaller and were decorated with swirling multi-coloured patterns.

The principle of the witch ball was that it was hung in the window of your house, to attract and neutralize the witch by its reflection of her evil eye or confusing her with its pattern.

Another variant of the witch ball recalls the Cambridgeshire witch bottle, as it was made of plain glass filled with small brightly coloured threads. If a witch ball went dull it meant there was infection in the air or a curse was being attempted at someone in the house. This is why they were also called watch balls, because you had to watch them and make sure they stayed shiny.

Today the effect of a witch ball as a reflector can be achieved with an appropriate Christmas tree decoration of a suitably reflective bauble hung in the window.

Witch Bottles

Under the doorstep and hearth are both common places to bury protective charms, such as a Witch Bottle. Witch bottles were a common protection in the Middle Ages, and whilst occasionally found under floors and walls, were predominantly buried under the hearth. They were made of glass (commonly blue, green or colourless) or the grey stoneware known as bellarmine (about two thirds of those found), commonly decorated with the face of a bearded man, and sealed with red or black wax.

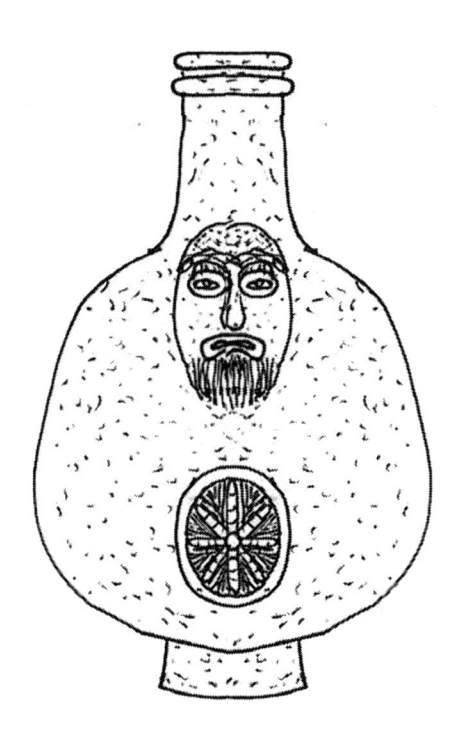

Certain ingredients seem to be universal in witch bottles, and others found in some of them. The universal (or nearly so) ingredients are human urine, and iron pins or nails. Common but not universal was human hair, salt, rosemary, semen and menstrual blood, thorns and small animal bones.

An examination of the substances added to witch bottles, which are specifically protective from malefic energies such as curses, may be beneficial here. Urine has been used since ancient times as a curse-breaking substance. This can be seen in ancient Egypt where it was viewed as a powerful repellent of demons and ghosts, and it has been used in this manner in many cultures since then. Urine is commonly used in Voodoo for example in curse-breaking, to break the magick of a cursed item by urinating on it. It may be that the power in urine is a combination of it being largely water, which has always been seen as magickal, with the fact that it is a waste product and therefore no longer has a magickal link to the body, and also it has a destructive quality due to the toxins in the urine which are being removed from the body. Another theory is that by sympathetic magick the curser would feel like they were *"pissing nails"* every time they went to the toilet.

Iron, as has been seen repeatedly throughout this book, is a common anti-magick material. It is believed to absorb or negate unwanted magickal power, and hence the frequent use of pins, nails, horseshoes, swords and other iron items for protection. Also, by using sharp items like nails and pins, there is the belief that they snag the negative energy and help trap and contain it.

Hair was probably added simply to create a magickal link between the person or people living in the house and the witch bottle, effectively keying the protection in to those whose hair was placed in the bottle. The same could be said of the semen and menstrual blood, though both these substances have strong anti-curse properties, being both believed to hold a very high magickal charge which would help negate any negative energy. Again this belief goes far back into the ancient world and can be seen in civilizations like ancient Egypt as well as indigenous cultures around the world.

Salt is known for its purificatory properties and is used in a number of anti-curse charms. Likewise rosemary is a classic anti-witch herb, often planted near the door to keep witches and their influence out. Thorns from trees like the blackthorn were widely used in charms for malefic magick, and so by including them in a witch bottle they could be seen as turning the witch's own tools against her. Animal bones are an interesting case, as they recall the burying of mummified cats under fireplaces and hearths. Also they would create a mixed magickal signature which could serve to confuse or deflect negative energies directed at the home.

Two other types of witch bottle need to be discussed, as they are ones I have encountered personally and are relevant to the area I grew up in. These are the Cambridgeshire witch bottle and the Trinity bottle. The Cambridgeshire witch bottle uses cord magick as the focus of its effectiveness. A small blue bottle is packed with small red threads measuring less than 3" (7.5cm) long. As each thread is individually packed into the bottle, the words of the empowering spell are spoken:

"Thread, tie up this sprite;
free us from its spite,
Tangle up the bane;
let not a piece remain."

The use of the threads is probably on the principle that they would entangle any negativity within their tangled mess. The red threads may also be seen in other charms such as the rowan and red thread. Also spirit lines or paths were sometimes represented with red cords or threads, which may have contributed to this usage.

The Trinity bottle is an old Cambridge fen form of portable witch bottle, made in the same way but using a triangular shaped iron bottle as the container for the ingredients (hence the name for the three sides). This would obviously be far more durable and less prone to breaking, making it a viable method of having a witch bottle on you when you are aware from the home.

Making your own Witch Bottle

Making a witch bottle is a simple process, and one you may wish to consider. If so, you should gather the following ingredients in preparation:

- ⊕ A suitable bottle, either bellarmine or if not then I recommend blue or green glass.
- ⊕ A red candle
- ⊕ An assortment of pins and nails. Ideally if they are a bit rusty this is good. Also you might consider burying them in your garden for a few days, so that they have a connection to the land around your home, which will further empower them for the purpose of protection.
- ⊕ Fresh rosemary herb, again preferably grown in your own garden if you have one.
- ⊕ Sea salt.
- ⊕ Some of your own urine, which you have collected.
- ⊕ A personal magickal link – this may be hair or semen or menstrual blood or nail clippings, whatever you prefer.

The different ingredients will serve the dual functions of making a magickal link to you for your protection, and also acting as a series of magickal boundaries and defences which keep the curse trapped. As the witch bottle works by a process of absorption of negative energy rather than deflection, it should be made on the new moon. The process is very simple.

- ⊕ Under the light of the new moon begin putting the ingredients in the bottle.
- ⊕ Start with the salt and rosemary, as these line the bottom nicely.
- ⊕ Add the nails and pins, which will then not clink on the bottom or have any chance of breaking it if they are heavy nails.
- ⊕ Add the personal magickal link and then add the urine.
- ⊕ Put the cork back in the bottle.
- ⊕ Light the red candle and drip the wax all around the top of the cork, sealing the bottle.

At this point I should mention that the first book to discuss the creation of a witch bottle also described destroying them to cause massive pain or even death to the witch. The book is Joseph Blagrave's *Astrological Practice of Physick*, published in 1657. In this work Blagrave advised slowly heating the witch bottle in a fire until it exploded, which would then allegedly cause the witch to be grieviously (or possibly mortally) injured, the extent of the injury perhaps matching the malevolence of the curse.

Magick Square Charm

An interesting amulet made on a triangular lead tablet makes use of the magick square of Saturn. A magick square is a number square, where all the rows, columns and diagonals add up to the same total. Each of the seven classical planets (Sun, Moon, Mercury, Venus, Mars, Jupiter and Saturn) has a magick square (also called a kamea), and traditionally these are used in amulets made on paper or parchment, or on tablets of the appropriate planetary metals. Each planet has a whole host of correspondences for magickal purposes, and the metals were frequently used for amulets. You will not be surprised to know that lead is the planetary metal of Saturn.

The version of this magick square that I have seen on a charm is actually slightly different to the one commonly reproduced in books and online, as the rows have the numbers in reverse to the popular one. This may be to emphasise the protective nature of the amulet, which is quite a simple charm to perform, and once made should be buried under the threshold or under the floorboards of the home. The magick square is thus:

2	9	4
7	5	3
6	1	8

And the method of its construction as explained to me by the charmer who taught me it is as follows:

- ⊕ On a Saturday, at sunrise, when Mercury is not retrograde, take your triangular piece of lead and a stylus for etching on it (note 3 is the number of Saturn and hence the triangle also represents its energy).

- ⊕ Draw the magick square onto the lead triangle, being sure to enclose the whole in a square, as above.

- ⊕ Now take the tablet and place it by a spider web so the spider can run over it. As soon as this has happened the charm is activated and ready to be used.

The spider connection here is an interesting one, which I have not come across elsewhere. I believe the underlying principle was a clear case of sympathetic magick, i.e. as a spider catches flies in its web, so will the charm be like a web to catch curses and negative energy. The spider running over the charm gives it a link to the spider and makes it akin to a magickal web. Obviously this charm is not for arachnophobes!

Chapter 6

Enlisting the Dead

"Free from human woes, beyond the power of death and harm."[7]

In the past what may be seen today as more gruesome methods were also resorted to for curse protection. One such technique was to place a horse skull in the fireplace or wall. This was a widespread practice as horses, like cats and dogs, were believed to be more sensitive to the invisible realms, and had a strength which could be drawn upon to protect from malefic influences. Horse skulls have even been found in church bell towers, and in one extreme instance, more than forty horse skulls were found screwed to the underside of the floor of a pub in Herefordshire. The association of horses with cursing may derive from our Norse ancestors, as it was a Norse practice to use a horse skull mounted on a long rune-carved staff for cursing, known as a niding staff or pole.

---

[7] On Purifications, Empedocles.

Dried cats have also been found in the walls, roofs and foundations of many old houses. These too, with their feline psychic sensitivity, were believed to protect the home from evil magick, and stop evil spirits from entering into the home they guarded. The ancient Egyptians used to mummify cats and other animals, but the purpose seems to have been very different. In the case of cats they had their necks broken and it was believed the spirit of the cat took a spell request with it to the cat goddess Bastet.

Some authors suggest the use of graveyard dust, i.e. earth taken from graves. Whilst this is frequently used in traditions like Voodoo, I strongly urge against such actions. Although there is undoubtedly power in such materials, it is a very strongly charged energy which can bring associations you do not want to include in your life. There is however one unusual church resident who can be very helpful in dealing with curses and cursers. This is the church grim.

The Church Grim Charm

A grim is an ethereal black dog, and a church grim is a particular form of grim, said to guard the souls of the dead in churchyards from the devil and witches. Unlike many other types of ethereal black dog he does not presage death and is not negative. A church grim appears as a large black dog with fiery eyes, sometimes seen peering out of churches late at night.

The following charm was related to me by an old man I met in Somerset. He recounted the charm as best he could remember it, with apologies for his faulty memory (he was in his nineties).

"Hie, Grim, come thee here
Gurt[8] beast dispel my fear
Send the witches down to hell
Help me now and toll the bell."

Obviously to use this charm you would need to look into folklore to see if there were any tales of a church grim in the area near you. Or if not you could always travel to the nearest one if you felt it was a charm you wished to try. Obviously it is encouraging the grim to deal with the curser in a very drastic manner, and so it is not a charm you should resort to lightly.

---

[8] Gurt is a local expression for great.

Chapter 7

Asking the Angels

"The Most high consigned the whole of mankind to the care of their own Angels for their preservation."[9]

Angels have become hugely popular in the modern world, indeed it might even be said that they are big business. This is somewhat ironic as the spiritual nature of angels is not automatically associated with capitalism, at least not in my mind. However in the past angels, like saints, were the workforce of the church, being called on by the populace to help solve problems, right wrongs, provide protection, blessings, etc. Thus it is no surprise that there should be charms with angels in.

One charm I have been shown is unusual in that it depicts the archangel Haniel on a red jasper cabochon, and must have required some skill on the part of the artisan who made it. Figures of gods and spirits carved on gems were common in the ancient world, as can be seen from visits to any good museum with a serious historical section. Dating has shown some medieval

---

[9] The Celestial Hierarchy, Pseudo-Dionysus the Areopagite

carved gems set into rings were actually Roman stones from centuries earlier being reused.

Haniel was the Venusian archangel, so his role as protector from curses would be as the power of victory (the meaning of Netzach, the Venusian sphere on the Qabalistic Tree of Life). Although I was surprised that it should have been Haniel rather than Michael, research did reveal that Haniel was particularly associated with red jasper, and that such a carved stone was believed to protect from phantasms and witchcraft, making it an ideal anti-curse stone. Also Haniel [pictured below] means *'Grace of God'*, so it does indicate seeking divine favour and protection, which is appropriate.

If you wished to reproduce this charm, my advice would be to paint the figure of Haniel on in fine gold, using something like a really fine 000 sable paintbrush. Obviously you do not have to use a cabochon, and could use a slice of the stone if you can find one as an alternative.

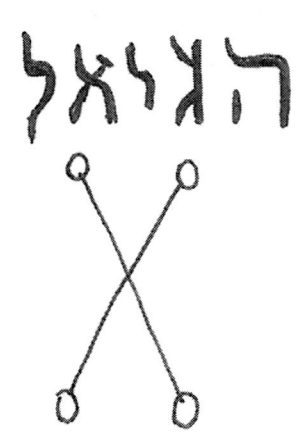

הגיאל

The symbols on the back of the charm [pictured above] are that of the name *Haniel* in Hebrew, and the figure is commonly found on charms since ancient times, and may symbolize balance, or even a version of the cross. Hebrew is of course written from right to left; hence the lettering reads LAINH when transliterated into the English equivalent.

Chapter 8

Quick Fixes

"If you have access to a kitchen, you are never defenceless."[10]

Sometimes you are away from your space and may need to increase the level of curse protection around yourself. Some old remedies can be used to help here. A classic charm is to put a bowl of vinegar in your room, to absorb any malefic energies. The principle behind this is probably that the acidity of the vinegar would attract and absorb any negativity directed towards the place.

Another charm which probably works on the same principle is to cut a lemon in half and leave that in the room with the face exposed to absorb any negativity. Other citrus fruits like lime, grapefruit or orange should also achieve the same effect, and indeed with its solar symbolism the orange might actually be preferable.

The other plant which is cut in half as a temporary protection is an onion. This is a classic technique, and it may be that the layers of the onion act as an effective

---

[10] Hilda Starling, private communication.

absorption tool, each additional layer adding to the protection.

A technique which has been borrowed into voodoo is to break a fresh egg at the place, as the release of the life energy is believed to act as a decoy for the curse. However this is only like to work if you are not specifically being targeted using a magickal link, when it will be a bit pointless.

Simply blessing some salt and water and making blessed water, to sprinkle around the room you are in will work adequately to keep malefic energies out in the short term, and does not require you to carry any special equipment. I would add that those little sachets of salt you get in fast food restaurants are very useful for this, and I always keep a couple in my wallet in case I need salt in a hurry.

Wearing a sprig of an anti-curse herb or flower is also a good temporary solution that does not need to attract too much attention. Something like rosemary, vervain or dill is ideal, or a flower like snapdragon.

There are various charms you could carry to provide protection when you are away from home, which I have discussed elsewhere. However as a quick and easy charm, obtain a belemnite to carry on you. Belemnite, also known as fairy fingers or thunderstone, is a traditional apotropaic charm, famous for its ability to deflect negative energy.

Cowrie shells too have a long history of being considered lucky, and in this sense can be worn as protection.

Alternatively, if you can find a piece of staurolite, also known as cross stone or fairy cross stone, this also has a strong reputation as a protective charm. Staurolite is distinctive in the cross pattern formed naturally on it, and the tale goes that the stones were formed from the tears of the fairy folk crying when they head of the crucifixion. This is a curious myth, until we recall some of the tales that suggest the fairies were originally the hidden children of Eve, or of Lucifer. As with all natural charms, the magick works better if you find them yourself, or if not that they are given in love. Buying such charms is not preferable, but if it is the only solution then that is what you do.

The pentagram, or *"druid's foot"*, is of course a classic protective symbol which you can use at any time. The ritual created by the Hermetic Order of the Golden Dawn known as the Lesser Banishing Ritual of the

Pentagram is a very effective way of protecting your space, and keeping any negative energies out. However as this is not a traditional protection from witchcraft, I shall not discuss it further, and encourage you to read one of the many books which describe how to practice this ritual if it interests you.

Nonetheless the power that has been invested in the pentagram for protection over the centuries is considerable, and it is a very good symbol to use, both as an instant protection and also for more enduring effects. A very useful technique when you are away from home is to bless some water as described elsewhere, and then draw pentagrams on any windows and doors to the space you are in with it. This then provides a magickal ward with a subtle physical basis, as the water will dry off, drawing the energy into the atmosphere of the room and charging the whole room with its protection. A similar principle can also be applied using essential oils, particularly ones which are essences of anti-cursing plants, but remember this is more noticeable from both the perspective of the smell and also the residue of the oil may leave stains on the window and door surfaces.

Chapter 9

Disconnection

"Upon the wicked he shall rain snares, fire and brimstone, and a horrible tempest, this shall be the portion of their cup."[11]

I mentioned earlier the ritual destruction of a magickal link placed in your space to facilitate a curse. This should be done in a manner which causes the maximum rebound of energies on the curser. After all, not only has this person cursed you, but they have abused your space as well! It also hopefully goes without saying that after dealing with such an item you would have no further contact with the person. Severing all contact with a person who has directed malice at you should always be a priority. Apart from in the workplace, there is no reason why you should maintain any contact with the individual. If they are likely to be in the same places as you , due to being connected to a mutual friend, then ignore them, and if necessary explain to the friend and be prepared to cut them loose too if they do

---

[11] Psalm 11:6.

not take you seriously and support you. Remember you have been wronged, and if people do not support you, they are not friends. You should not have to change your patterns or hide away simply because some sad idiot decided in a fit of jealousy to curse you.

Destroying Magickal Links

So back to the destruction of magickal links. The method I am including here is quite drastic and not for the faint hearted, and is based on Grimoire material. If it is too extreme for you, simply immerse the magickal link in a bowl of salt for a period of time like a week, and then bury it somewhere far away from your home, or preferably throw it into a river or the sea.

But if you want to send the negative energy back to the curser to short-circuit their malice, then this is the procedure for you:

- ⊕ Put the magickal link in a cardboard box, filled with feathers, brimstone (sulphur), rue, vervain and dill.

- ⊕ In a suitable outdoor space, away from people, prepare a fire. Be sure to choose a place where you will not be troubled by park rangers or other such people telling you off for lighting a fire in a no-fire zone. They might suddenly become very interested in what you are doing, and you really do not want to explain this one!

- ⊕ Burn the box containing the link on the fire, keeping your distance, as it will smell awful.

When you have finished, gather any remnants of the magickal link that have not burned, and take them to the nearest river and throw them in. The running water will complete the break of contact very well.

Chapter 10

Return to Sender

"Doomed to perish swiftly like smoke they are carried aloft and wafted away."[12]

Protecting yourself from a curse is a good start, but I am a great believer in returning the energy a person puts out to them. If they are sending you negativity, reflect it to them and let them have a taste of their own medicine. The best way to ensure somebody does not make the same mistake of directing negativity at you is to switch the tables so they receive what they were trying to give.

At this point I should state that I am not a Wiccan and therefore do not believe in the Wiccan law of threefold return. I believe in the principle of action and reaction. Any action creates a reaction, so if someone acts to cause negativity towards me, they should expect a reaction in equal measure. There is a place for passivity and a place for action. If someone is acting maliciously towards you or your loved ones, there is no time for passivity, only for stamping out their malevolence. To

---

[12] On Nature, Empedocles.

this end we shall consider ways to reflect energy back in this chapter, which may seem harsh in places. Whether you choose to use any of these techniques is a matter for you and your beliefs. I am a great believer in making the tools to do a good job available, if someone chooses not to use all the tools that is their choice.

You may have seen books or articles where the writers recommend that you be in a state of anger to deal with the curse, as that is as near an equivalent emotion to the negative state of the curser as you can get (hatred, jealousy, etc). Alternatively some writers suggest fighting the curse with love, to transform it. I would say that both of these approaches are wrong. You should be in a calm and balanced state, and not off balance through an excess of any emotion, be it positive or negative.

Consider being angry – it can raise energy, but it means that you are probably not going to be as focused as you could be, and also that you may allow yourself to do things that you later regret but seemed a good idea at the time. Conversely, the New Age approach of transforming with love is quite nonsensical. To illustrate, if we consider this from an elemental point of view, love corresponds to water, and hate to fire. Elements can only be transformed into those they share qualities with, not their opposites. Fire and water are direct opposites from an elemental perspective and cannot be transformed into each other. Water does not burn with a flame (yes it may scald as steam, but it is then hot airy water).

The folklore associated with peacock feathers spans both good and bad. Peacocks used to be considered a symbol of Christ, but this was turned around and they were sometimes seen as a symbol of the devil, demonstrating the sin of vanity in their display behaviour. However the colourful feather with the eye on the end also has an association with reflecting the evil eye. Ignore the modern superstition about it being unlucky to bring peacock feathers into your home – it is an excellent reflector, and more subtle than most charms as it can be easily explained away to curious guests.

Moving from peacock to peacock stone, malachite also has along history of use to avert the evil eye, due to the patterns found in the black lines which permeate the beautiful green colour of the stone. Traditionally it is particularly used to protect babies, with a piece of malachite being hung above the baby's cot to protect it from the evil eye.

An amulet which people are completely unaware of and which can be found in many country homes is the horse brass. These were originally worn by horses to reflect the evil eye. Now they adorn public houses and homes, with people completely unaware of their protective qualities. So for an amulet which can look good and serve its function, the horse brass is a good choice. When you polish it, so it is as reflective as possible, you should do so in a clockwise direction, and be thinking of its protective qualities at the same time. That way you are investing some energy into it and also effectively programming it as an amulet to protect your space.

As previously mentioned, salt is a great purifying substance. It is used in modern magick by ceremonial magicians and Wiccans and others, but traditionally was used against witches. A handful of salt thrown into the fire was believed to torment witches and drive them away. In Lancashire it was believed this should be done to break bewitchments, for nine successive mornings with the words: *"Salt, salt, put thee into the fire, and may the person who has bewitched me neither eat, drink, nor sleep, till the spell is broken."*

Although it is not a traditional British method, I have decided to include a Florentine witch's curse breaking method. This is because it illustrates a number of points well, using many of the basic magickal principles very effectively. The technique runs as follows.

Powdered cumin and a Martial incense were cast onto hot coals and stabbed and stirred vigorously with a sharp knife. Each room in the house in turn would be fumigated, with the chant: *"I do not stab the incense, but rather the body, soul and all the feelings of the wretched person who has sent ill-fortune to my house!"* When this was done, a yellow slip of paper and two iron nails (wired together as an equal-armed cross) were both thrown onto the red-hot coals.

If you did not know who had made the curse, the coals, ash and cross were thrown into a stream or river (running water). If you did know, they were to be buried under the eves of his roof (i.e. on his property so the effect was rebounded).

Looking at this practice we can see the use of a spice, with its inner heat, combined with a Martial incense to create the sympathetic link to the curser. Although perhaps unusual as a technique, the smoke is being used as a menstruum or basis for the transmission. This may be because the incense, being airy, would be dispersed into the local area, where undoubtedly the curser lived. It is one of those unspoken universal principles that a person almost always curses someone familiar. In the past this would have been somebody who lived in the same area, now it may be the same workplace.

The systematic fumigation of the house, with the chant repeated in each room, is similar to the principle of exorcism, ensuring that there is nowhere for the negative energy to take hold by forcing it out. The slip of paper would presumably have the name of the suspect on if known, or otherwise something to symbolize the curser. This would burn on the coals, again indicating a resolution of the action and breaking the magickal link. The almost inevitable use of iron is seen in the form of the cross formed of two nails, which add the power of the religious symbolism to the rite, further empowering it.

The disposal of the coals and other items into running water shows a final affirmation that the curse is well and truly broken, as running water is well known for its ability to resist magick. The alternative of putting the bits on the property of the curser shows the determination to ensure payback is delivered.

The use of lead curse tablets (called *defixiones*) in the ancient world has been well documented. Small lead tablets would have the curse inscribed on them and then often have nails hammered through them. The tablets were usually dropped into wells or buried in the earth, putting the tablets into the underworld, which was generally perceived as being the home of malefic magick.

This is why curses and protection from curses was particularly associated with chthonian deities like the Egyptian Anubis and Greek Hekate. This technique continued through into witchcraft, with the tablet sometimes being replaced with a poppet, and has also been used for curse and spell breaking charms as well.

The following figure, which was shown to me by a Cornish Pellar (charmer) some years ago, should be drawn on a lead tablet.

The pellar who showed me it was an archaeologist by trade, and took great delight in pointing out similarities between this charm and similar ones found in healing spas and wells like those at the Roman baths in Bath near Bristol here in England. Obviously the Hebrew divine names (Eheieh, Adonai, Agla and Elohim) are not

87

something that would be found in such ancient charms, though they were popular in charms made from the Middle Ages onwards. The use of divine names which all start with the letter A (aleph in Hebrew) may be connected with the use of the Latin quote, *"In principio erat verbum"* from John 1:1,[13] as it is the first letter, and so is there in the beginning, as it were. That the names are written left to right shows they were not written by a Jew. The use of the ouroboros serpent is interesting, and seems akin in this instance to a magick circle around the divine names. The equal-armed cross was a standard inclusion in charms and magick circles alike.

Applying standard magickal principles, this charm should be made on a waxing moon, though it could be made in daylight under the light of the sun for a more apotropaic quality. The piece of lead should be obtained without haggling and cut into a square shape. Due to its soft nature lead is easy to shape. The charm should be kept in the house for protection.

For amulets which protect from curses, the deities called on are almost inevitably either solar gods of light (such as Abraxas as seen earlier) or sometimes magick gods, such as Hekate and Anubis, who also have a chthonian underwordly aspect as well. The divine names used on such amulets are usually Hebrew divine names (see above) or Greek barbarous words, which were often palindromes or strings of letters or words.

---

[13] "In the beginning was the word."

Chapter 11

Poppets

"When these (elements) have been mixed in the form of a man and come into the light."[14]

A poppet, also sometimes called a fith-fath or fetch, is a human simulacrum made to represent a particular individual. Although there are instances recorded of a doll being used for this purpose, it is generally perceived as being more efficacious if the poppet is made by the person performing the curse.

Of course poppets can also be used for binding a person, to stop them from cursing, which is what we are more concerned with here. The process of making a poppet is not difficult, and they can be very effective if you know the identity of the person cursing you.

---

[14] On Nature, Empedocles.

To make a poppet you will require:

- A piece of white cotton, at least 2' x 1' (60cm x 30cm)
- A needle and some white cotton thread
- A good supply of herbs to stuff it with
- Permanent ink pens to mark and decorate the poppet

The process is a simple one, and is best performed at the full moon. You need to decide what sort of herb to fill your poppet with, personally I think vervain is a good choice. If you go back to the section entitled *The Protective Garden* there is plenty to choose from there. Remember that whatever herb you use it should be properly dried so it does not rot whilst it is in the poppet, unless that is what you intend for it to do of course. The process of constructing the poppet is:

- Fold the piece of cotton in half so it is square, and then mark on a person shape.

- Cut the shape out, giving you two identical person shaped pieces of cotton.

- Sew the two shapes together, leaving the top of the head open, so there is enough room for you to stuff the poppet with herbs to give it body.

- ⊕ When you have finished stuffing the poppet sew the head up so it is completely sewn together and will not leak herbs.

- ⊕ Draw a face on to represent the curser. Obviously you should use colours as close as possible to their eye and hair colour to make it resemble the curser more.

If you have anything of the persons to use as a magickal link, this should either be placed inside the poppet if it is a body link like hair or nail, or attached to the poppet if it is a photo or piece of cloth or jewellery or some such. Note if you have a photo you can cut the face out and put it on the face of the poppet to make it an exact representation of the curser.

Now you have made the poppet you need to activate it and bind it to prevent the curser from acting against you. I would suggest the waning half moon as the best time to do this. At this point the moon is waning, indicating restriction, but the moon is in a state of balance of light and dark, indicating the non-malefic nature of your binding, i.e. that it is done for a positive reason and not out of malice.

A simple ceremony will suffice to activate the poppet and bind it.

For this you will need:

⊕ Elemental representations – incense for air, a red candle for fire, a bowl of water for water and a bowl of earth for earth. Note a purificatory incense like frankincense or myrrh resin or sandalwood or pine would be good to use. If it is warranted, you may choose to add a banishing herb like St John's Wort or Hyssop.

⊕ Three lengths of red thread for binding the poppet with.

⊕ Prepare your altar or table, light the incense and candle. You will need to be extra careful when passing the poppet through the candle flame, as you do not want to singe or burn the poppet.

Procedure:

⊕ Pass the poppet through the incense, saying *"Air gave you breath."*

⊕ Pass the poppet through the candle flame, saying *"Fire gave you spirit."*

⊕ Sprinkle the poppet with water, saying *"Water made your blood."*

⊕ Sprinkle the poppet with earth, saying *"Earth made your bones."*

⊕ Blow into the mouth of the poppet, saying *"With the breath of life I name you [name of curser]."*

⊕ Wrap the first length of red thread around the body of the poppet, binding the arms and especially hands to the body, saying *"I bind you [name of curser] from acting harmfully towards me."*

⊕ Wrap the second length of red thread around the mouth of the poppet, saying *"I bind you [name of curser] from speaking ill of me or directing malefic words towards me."*

⊕ Wrap the third length of red thread around the head of the poppet, saying *"I bind you [name of curser] from directing malefic intent towards me."*

The poppet should then be stored in a secure place, and left there. When the time comes that you feel the person has no more ill intent towards you, you may if you choose deconsecrate the poppet. The easiest way to do this is to remove the red threads and destroy them, and to simply bury the poppet.

Chapter 12

Caught in the Act

"The overconfident underachieve."[15]

In the rare event that you actually catch somebody in the act of cursing you, there are several approaches you can take. Of course you need to be sure that is what is going on, but there is a distinct miasma of negativity around somebody seeking to curse you or hex you with the Evil Eye. A traditional approach is to spit in the direction of the person three times, and then walk away ignoring them. This is an act of belittlement, combined with the apotropaic power of saliva. In some primitive cultures the more extreme act of urinating towards the person replaces spitting, but this is not something that is likely to be acceptable in today's world!

Visualising a mirror in front of yourself to bounce the negativity back towards the person is an obvious technique. If you want to be a bit more obvious and also gain the psychological high ground, draw a pentagram in

---

[15] Hilda Starling, private communication.

the air in front of yourself and then push it towards them with a dramatic gesture. They will be so busy in their paranoia trying to protect themselves that their cursing attempt will be broken and temporarily forgotten, and you can then depart knowing that any future attempt will be riddled with doubt and doomed to failure.

What I say next will sound extremely paranoid, but it is part of the principle of magickal insurance. If you carry a small white quartz pebble around on you, this makes an ideal spirit trap, and can be used to trap the negative energy the person directs at you. The pebble should not be any old pebble, rather I refer to the ones that are often to be found at old burial mounds. These are imbued with the energy of the place, and have a link both to death and the ancestors, making a potent combination. This is why they are often used as charms, as quartz makes an excellent battery, holding magickal charge very well. This is a charm you have to go and find, you cannot buy it at a shop or online or at a psychic fair. Remember too that the effort of going and finding such a charm will already have given it extra power.

So if somebody is cursing you, take out your quartz pebble and see all the negativity they are sending at you like a stream of dirty grey being absorbed into the pebble. If you can manage it, smile at the person the whole time, as again this will disturb their equilibrium and give you more of an advantage. Once the situation is over, in your eyes, take your leave and go to the nearest graveyard and bury the quartz pebble there. You have then effectively made a sort of *"magnetic"* locus, which will draw and earth the energy the curser directs at you. As the energy is effectively being earthed with the energy of death, the curser may find that their health starts to deteriorate the more they curse you, as the pebble will act like a sort of black hole, sucking all the energy they direct into it, and leaving them drained. Such is the fate that people who curse you deserve.

Chapter 13

Cleansing & Setting Wards

"I have flown out of the Circle of Heavy Grief and stepped swift-footed on the Circle of Joy."[16]

One of the times in your life when the greatest disconnection occurs is of course house moving. When you move house, you have the perfect opportunity to not only get rid of old clutter, but also to ensure that your new home is thoroughly protected from any negative influence. Of course you should make sure that the new house is psychically clean first, and a good banishing to ensure that the house is in a neutral state is always recommended.

Living in Somerset as I do, I am very aware that some old houses come with their own ethereal residents. If you are moving in to an older property, you might want to check there are no ethereal beings already in residence. If there are, you need to decide whether you are going to accept them or get rid of them. A hostile

---

[16] Bacchic Gold Tablet A1-3, 5th century BCE.

ethereal being in your space can be as bad or worse than being cursed, as they are in your space all the time, and it is nigh on impossible to hide anything from them as you can from a person cursing you.

Firstly let us look at the positive side of things. Unless the people are leaving the property because the ethereal being has made their lives hell, the chances are that it will be tied in with the property and will be perfectly amenable if approached courteously. In such circumstances they can be enlisted to be an ethereal guardian to your home, and will be a strong ally against any sort of negative attack. If the entity was particularly attached to the previous owners, then it may well leave with them to go to their new home. Once the boundaries are defined there should be no problems, think of it like a contract between you and the ethereal being.

The negative side would be if the entity takes a dislike to you and starts trying to interfere in your life. This would be likely to manifest through things going missing, accidents and breakages, disturbed sleep due to unexpected noises, and other disturbances. In such circumstances you should get rid of the being. Find somebody competent to banish the being from your house. I am not going to go into the details here, as it is a process which requires a great deal of experience to do well and could fill a whole book by itself.

So let us deal with the issue of how to deal with a welcome house guest of the ethereal kind! Well, regular offerings left in the room it seems to prefer are a good move, usually simply water or food like bread are good. Trust your instincts and offer what feels right. Make an effort to contact the being and mentally establish a connection and let it know how you want things done. Beyond that, explain that you are going to do a complete clean of the house but that it is not included in the psychic blasting you are about to unleash.

To neutralize the energy of the house, you should go round and purify each room in the house in turn, in a systematic manner. Use blessed water and also a good purifying incense. I would suggest either simply burning a resin like frankincense, or else making a blend if you feel confident in your ability to do so. Four parts frankincense with one part each of hyssop and St Johns Wort is a good combination. Remember that your censer should have some earth in it before lighting the charcoal, to absorb heat so it is easy to carry comfortably from room to room without getting too hot. Take your bowl of blessed water and censer of incense to each room and sprinkle and cense the room, repeating the following chant:

"Earth and water, fire and air
Banish and cleanse and strip it bare."

This is a simple chant I wrote, with the elements in what would be seen as an anticlockwise sequence if looking at the common modern magickal attributions on the magick circle. Repeat the chant as you go from room to room, so that it is an unbroken litany. This may result in you saying it many dozens of times, but that is good and fine. You can of course make up your own chant instead, mine is simply an example of the sentiment you should be expressing. Before you leave a room, draw pentagrams on the doors and windows and walls, floor and ceiling with the blessed water. This then ensures that the room is temporarily sealed whilst you are in the rest of the house and nothing will come in after you have moved away leaving it blank.

When you have finished, start using whichever of the techniques you prefer from this book to protect the space. You might put charms over the windows or main doors, such as a horseshoe over the front door, or rowan and red thread charms, or hagstones, or a witch ball in the window. The choice is entirely yours. Remember that the more secure you make your home, the less chance there is of any negativity getting in. At the same time, if it is completely festooned with charms hanging from every door, window and rafter, it could cause a lot of funny looks!

Chapter 14

Herbal Sprinkler; Holy Water

"Water is a symbol of life."[17]

In the most famous of all Grimoires, the *Key of Solomon*, instructions are given on how to make a herbal sprinkler which contains most of the aforementioned herbs. Reference is made to the time of construction, which should be during the planetary hours of Mercury on a Wednesday during a waxing moon. The timing is the same as for the construction of the hazel wand, which is not surprising as a piece of hazel is used as the basis of the sprinkler:

"Thou shalt then make unto thyself a Sprinkler of vervain, fennel, lavender, sage, valerian, mint, garden-basil, rosemary, and hyssop, gathered in the day and hour of Mercury, the moon being in her increase. Bind together these herbs with a thread spun by a young maiden, and

---

[17] Timaeus, Proclus.

engrave upon the handle on the one side the following characters"

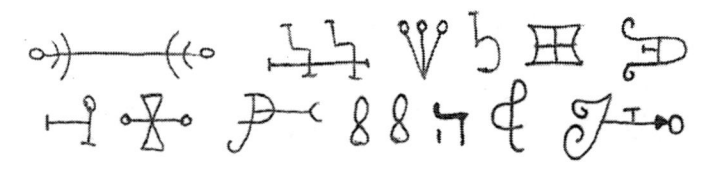

Above: Front of the Sprinkler Wand
Below: Back of the Sprinkler Wand

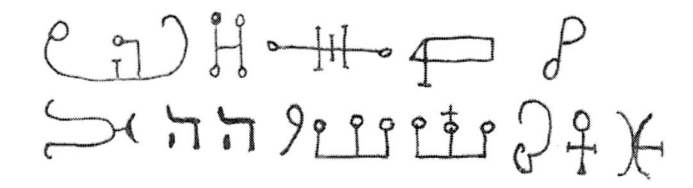

"After this thou mayest use the Water, using the Sprinkler whenever it is necessary; and know that wheresoever thou shalt sprinkle this Water, it will chase away all Phantoms, and they shall be unable to hinder or annoy any. With this same Water thou shalt make all the preparations of the Art."

Of course you also need to be able to make holy or blessed water to use the sprinkler. You do not have to be a priest to do this, as anyone can make holy water. However you can of course go and take some from your local church if you prefer.

To make holy water place the salt and the water into two separate bowls ready. First say these words over the salt:

"Tzabaoth Messiach, Emanuel, Elohim Gibor, Yod He Vav He; O God, Who art the Truth and the Life, bless and sanctify this Creature of salt to serve me for protection."

Then cast the salt into the water and say the following words from Psalm 6:7-10 as you stir it in:

"Mine eye is consumed because of grief; it waxeth old because of all mine enemies. Depart from me, all ye workers of iniquity; for the Lord hath heard the voice of my weeping. The Lord hath heard my supplication; the Lord will receive my prayer. Let all mine enemies be ashamed and sore vexed; let them return and be ashamed suddenly."

Purists will notice the words I give are slightly adapted from those in the *Key of Solomon*. This is because they are being used for the specific protective purpose against curses, rather than for consecrating magick circles for evocation and the like. Although some people keep their blessed water for subsequent use, personally I recommend making fresh every time. Any spare can always be used to strengthen wards on the house.

CHAPTER 15

Curse Justification

"Avert from my tongue the madness of those men."[18]

The question has to be asked, can you ever be justified in resorting to a curse yourself. This is an ethical question that can only be decided by you. As I have already made clear throughout this book, I do not believe in turning the other cheek and being a passive victim. Bullies, whatever their type, should get some of their own medicine in my opinion. Sometimes it can cure them and do everybody a favour. At the least it makes them think twice about trying to pick on you again. It should be clear that many of the techniques I have described can be adapted and used to curse somebody if needed. However I can only comment that in my opinion curses should only be resorted to when all other methods fail. I would have no problem with cursing a criminal who has got off with their crime and not been punished,

---

[18] On Nature, Empedocles.

if the crime is one that has caused a person to suffer and will leave lasting emotional scars.

You may say, surely you are no better than the person who cursed you if you too resort to curses. This is not true, as it is all about intent. There is a great difference between cursing somebody malevolently out of jealousy and malice, than cursing somebody to ensure they pay for their negative actions. It is up to you to decide whether this is something for you or not.

If you do decide that you need to take such action against somebody who has caused unpleasant personal damage, then you should not pussyfoot around, but commit yourself to the course of action. A simple curse you can use, which I was told by a friend who is a ceremonial magician, is the cat litter curse. This is very easy and requires very little effort on your part, though you do need to have a cat. You simply write the person's name on a piece of paper, or preferably on a photograph of them. Then put the paper/photo in the bottom of your cat litter tray. Every time you cat goes to the toilet, it is literally dumping on the person on a psychic level, encouraging their life to *"turn to crap"*, as it were! Remembering the earlier discussion of the magickal properties of urine, it can be seen that this is simply an inversion of the ancient Egyptian practice of putting a person's name on a piece of meat or in a piece of bread which was fed to a cat. The Egyptians believed that the cat goddess Bastet would magickally attack the person, reflecting on a universal scale the action of the cat eating the food.

A variation of this is to engrave the person's name on a piece of lead and place it in the sole of your shoe so that every step you take you are treading on them. This serves the magickal purpose of belittling any negative energy they are directing towards you, as it will effectively be drawn down to the lead sheet and earthed as you walk. Hence this technique can work as a sort of lightning rod at the same time, dispelling any negative energy directed at you if you believe the person is cursing you.

A technique which was commonly used in the past to break a curse was to draw the blood of the curser, which would immediately negate their curse. Of course this did assume that you knew who the curser was. All that was needed was a scratch, and then as now to had to be done carefully or you could be charge for assault. Also of course, in this day and age you need to bear in mind if you do scratch a person to make sure that you do not have any cuts or scratches on your hands, as you do not want to risk being infected with any disease that is transferable through blood. This is not something that can be realistically done unless you know the person, and even then it would need to be staged carefully if you were going to do it.

Chapter 16

Passive Curses

"As for any man ... who shall remove this book ... their corpse shall not be buried ... their name shall not be remembered anywhere on earth"[19]

A passive curse is one which is activated by a specific action. The most common form of passive curse is one which is activated by theft. So when an item is stolen, the curse is activated and directed at the thief. Passive curses have been around for thousands of years, and have a particularly strong connection with books and manuscripts. Ancient Sumerian and Egyptian priests lay curses on their books to ensure terrible things happened to anyone who dared to steal them. This technique continued well into the Middle Ages, with scribes writing curses in to manuscripts, often in the colophon at the back. Even today some authors are returning to the practice of putting curses in their material for any who

---

[19] Extract from a passive book curse, Bremner-Rhind Papyrus.

abuse their information through pirating, be it in book or electronic form.

I know magicians who have put these passive curses not only on books, but also on their magickal paraphernalia. This is of course understandable, but personally I have nothing that I am so attached to that I wish to put a passive curse on it. Whether this idea appeals to you and you wish to explore it further is in your hands. Remember though if you do decide to apply such passive curses to warn any friends who borrow your books, especially those who can be a bit tardy in returning them!

CHAPTER 17

Closing Thoughts

"Speech is the echo of the thought in the soul."[20]

By now you may be slightly agog at the amount of curse-connected material you have read about. Bear in mind this is only material that comes from the time I have spent speaking to the elders who were willing to talk to someone with a willing ear, and looking through libraries, it is by no means comprehensive. I may be viewed as a Luddite, but frankly I do not feel the avalanche of technology that has buried modern society has been a progressive step. We are in danger of stepping too far away from our roots and the land. Values which seem almost archaic, like honour, courtesy and community can still be found if you look in the right places, and will never die as long as people are true to themselves and their environment.

---

[20] Enneads, Plotinus,

Plotinus, writing in his *Enneads* on Beauty, describes inflicted ugliness in terms akin to being cursed. He wrote:

"If a man has been immersed in filth or daubed in mud, his native comeliness disappears and all that is seen is the foul stuff besmearing him: his ugly condition is due to alien matter that has encrusted him, and if he is to win back his grace it must be his business to scour and purify himself and make himself what he was."

When I started writing this book it was to preserve knowledge, but it has become clear to me that it is also about self-knowledge. Although being cursed is not a pleasant experience, it can force you to reassess your life and be more focused, as implied by the quote I have given above. I hope that you purchased this book because you were interested in the material and wanted it as an insurance policy, in case you are ever cursed, rather than already being the recipient of a curse. Either way, if the material has made you think about how you interact with nature, whether you waste your energy on people and activities that do not serve any useful purpose, or prompted you to want to learn more about an area of magick, then I will have achieved the goals I realised were hidden in the words waiting to manifest. May your gods bless you with happiness, and may you bless the land with your thoughtfulness and care.

APPENDIX

(I) Picking Herbs Properly

As a magickal herbalist at this point I would like to add some advice on how to pick herbs in the most magickally effective way for use in protection, or any other purpose for that matter. Traditionally herbs are most commonly picked on the new or full moon, or on specific days of the year thought to mark particular energetic tides, such as Roodmas Eve and St John's Day. When you pick a herb it should be treated as a solemn act, entered into with full intent and respect for the plant. To pick a plant for protective use follow these guidelines, which have been adhered to for centuries by herbalists and root-cutters and have both symbolic and traditional associations:

Never use iron, a stick or piece of horn or even a copper tool is okay if you need to dig the plant out for its roots. In such circumstances dig very carefully so as not to damage the plant unduly.

Use your non-dominant hand to pick with. For most people this will be their left hand. If you are ambidextrous use the hand you do not normally write with. By using the non-dominant hand you are signaling the subtle use of the plant. If you were picking for healing you could use your dominant hand, as this symbolizes the desire for a physical effect as opposed to a subtle one.

If possible be barefoot to have a stronger connection to the earth.

The ideal is to wear a white cotton robe, but as this is not practical for many people, natural fabrics are preferred, and white is also best.

Explain to the plant before you pick it why you are doing so, and make a small offering to show you are exchanging energies. This can be some food, like bread or fruit, or milk and honey is a good traditional offering. Coins were also frequently offered and buried. If I can work out the age of the plant, I offer a coin minted in the same year as the plant's birth. Note please do not offer crystals, this is a New Age practice that stems from wooly thinking and does not achieve anything except perpetuating the unnecessary purchase of crystals. Putting a crystal that comes from an entirely different part of the world, with different energetic connections, into the earth is like introducing a foreign species into the ecosystem, it can disrupt the energies around it. An even worse example is when people leave such offerings at stone circles, which do not want amethysts or rose quartz shoved in them, thank you very much!

Once the plant is picked, it should go into a receptacle you have ready for the purpose, and not touch the ground again, as this is believed to drain the power of the plant back into the earth. I would recommend having either a leather satchel or basket lined with a piece of white cotton, which you can put the plant straight into.

Remember to thank the plant after picking it. Don't worry about feeling silly, it marks a resolution of the process, and the chances are you will be picking your herbs when nobody is around to see you anyway.

If you are picking twigs or branches from a tree, you need to be even more respectful. Remember the tree is probably much older than you, and seen a lot more too. Approach the tree slowly, not hurrying, and when you are standing a couple of yards away from it, explain what you need the wood for. The chances are that you will feel a sense of acceptance, in which case you can proceed. Occasionally you might feel a distinct sense of being unwelcome. If this occurs, whatever you do, do not pick a piece of the tree as it is clearly telling you it will not willingly part with a piece of itself, and whatever you pick will not be energetically positive for your work. Also you will have annoyed a tree spirit and this could result in the area around it becoming much less friendly to you in future.

Before breaking or cutting off a branch or twig, stroke towards the trunk of the tree at the break point, seeing the energy separate out. See the energy like golden sap inside the tree, and visualize a distinct gap at the break point, so the break occurs in a way that no energy leaks out of the tree or the piece you are gathering. After making the cut or break, stroke the area and see it sealed. You can rub a bit of your saliva into the break on the tree as an offering if you wish.

As before, always thank a tree and make an offering, which should be left at the base of the trunk if food, or poured if it is liquid.

Although it is obvious, I will re-emphasise that offerings should be made of food products which are native to your country.

(II) Empedocles' Elements

The Greek root cutter and philosopher Empedocles (c. 490-430 BCE) is one of the greatest contributors to the development of modern magick. He has been largely ignored until the last few years, and is now starting to get the attention he deserves. His ideas are fundamental and should be mentioned to qualify the underlying philosophy behind the way I work and write.

In his classic work *Tetrasomia* (Doctrine of the Four Elements), Empedocles set out the doctrine of the four elements, which would underlie the subsequent magickal traditions for the next two and a half thousand years to the current day. As well as his doctrine of the four elements, Empedocles also postulated two opposing divine forces which act throughout the universe, love and strife. These divine forces represent the powers of attraction and repulsion. From this you can see why I should want to write about dealing with curses, which embody an imbalance towards strife.

	North	
Cold	Earth	Dry
West Water		East Fire
Moist	Air South	Warm

An important aspect of the doctrine of the four elements is the way the elements interact. Each element has two main qualities, and an element can be transformed into another element with which it shares a quality, being those on either side of it. This means that opposing elements cannot be transformed into each other, i.e. Fire and Water cannot be transformed into each other, and neither can Air and Earth. As can be seen from the illustration above of the Elemental Square, the attributions of Air and Fire to the directions used in modern magick are different to those given by Empedocles.

Further Reading

If you have enjoyed this work and wish to learn more, I would recommend the following works, which were of greater or lesser relevance to the material I have covered within.

Betz, Hans Dieter (ed); *The Greek Magical Papyri in Translation*; 1992; University of Chicago Press, Chicago

Blake, Margaret; *Discovering the Folklore of Plants*; 1999; Shire Publications Ltd; Buckinghamshire

Davies, Owen; *Cunning-Folk: Popular Magic in English History*; 2003; Hambledon and London; London

Gager, John G.; *Curse Tablets and Binding Spells from the Ancient World*; 1992; Oxford University Press; Oxford

Huson, Paul; *Mastering Witchcraft*; 1970; Perigree Books; New York

Mathers, S.L. MacGregor (trans); *The Key of Solomon the King (Clavicula Salomonis)*; 1889; Redway; London

Merrifield, Ralph; *The Archaeology of Ritual Magic*; 1987; B.T. Batsfield Ltd; London

Mullins, Rose; *White Witches: A Study of Charmers*; 2000; P.R. Publishing; Cornwall

Nottingham, G St. M.; *Charms Charming & the Charmed: Welsh Border Witchcraft*; 2007; Verdelet Press; Shropshire

CPSIA information can be obtained at www.ICGtesting.com
Printed in the USA
LVOW132222291012

304895LV00001B/7/P

9 781905 297184